Careers
Working with
Children and
Young People

Careers Working with Children and Young People

SEVENTH EDITION

JUDITH HUMPHRIES

First published in 1981
Second edition 1984
Both entitled *Careers Working With Children*
Seventh edition 1996

Apart from any fair dealing for the purposes of research or private study, or criticism or review, as permitted under the Copyright, Designs and Patents Act, 1988, this publication may only be reproduced, stored or transmitted, in any form or by any means, with the prior permission in writing of the publishers, or in the case of reprographic reproduction in accordance with the terms of licences issued by the Copyright Licensing Agency. Enquiries concerning reproduction outside those terms should be sent to the publishers at the undermentioned address:

Kogan Page Limited
120 Pentonville Road
London N1 9JN

© Kogan Page Limited 1981, 1984, 1987, 1989, 1992, 1994, 1996

British Library Cataloguing in Publication Data

A CIP record for this book is available from the British Library.

ISBN 0-7494-1928-8

Typeset by DP Photosetting, Aylesbury, Bucks
Printed and bound in Great Britain by
Clays Limited, St Ives plc

Contents

Part 2

Part 1

Introduction

Children certainly capture the imagination and engage the emotions of most people, but is a ready response to their more appealing aspects enough to make somebody suitable for working with them?

This century has seen great changes in people's attitudes to children. A hundred years ago, people thought that 'children should be seen and not heard'. Children from poor families were sent, as young as ten years old, to work in factories or in the fields, and the children of the rich had to learn tedious and detailed lessons in their schools and academies or with tutors and governesses. Today many people feel that the pendulum has swung too far the other way and that there is too much freedom and too little discipline. Whether you agree with this or not, if you wish to work with children you will need to understand the reasons for the great changes which have taken place.

The most important influence on our attitude to children has been the growth of two subjects: psychology, or the study of the mind, and sociology, the study of society and the way it works. From these came a new understanding of child development and of the factors likely to lead to normal or satisfactory growth from babyhood to adulthood. We now see children as individuals, each with his or her own personality and potential which, given the right conditions, can be encouraged and developed. We realise that health, happiness and an ability to get along with other people are just as important as academic learning and so a variety of new provisions has been made to cater for these needs.

The Scope of this Book

Teaching is still the single largest career for people wanting to work with children - the field is so wide, in fact, that it needs a book to itself (see *Careers in Teaching* by Felicity Taylor, in this series). This book details the opportunities available for people who want to work with children outside school, in playgroups and nurseries, residential homes and day centres, and with young people during their leisure activities. There are also schools where the teachers need some assistance, mainly infant schools and schools for the handicapped; jobs in these institutions are also described. There is a section on non-medical work with children in hospital. (Those interested in the medical care of sick children should consult *Careers in Nursing and Related Professions* by Linda Nazarko.)

Part 1 deals with the jobs themselves and Part 2 with the courses of training which you can take to prepare for them.

Do not imagine for one moment that working with children is the perfect way to avoid growing up yourself. If you intend to work with children you need to be very mature, as most jobs involve constantly taking decisions and using your own initiative. You must also be able to communicate well with adults and with children, as you will often be required to sort out misunderstandings between the two. Many of the courses detailed in this book require you to have had some practical experience with children before beginning your studies. This kind of experience can usually be gained by doing voluntary work which may be full or part time – see Chapter 5.

Most of the jobs we are dealing with are not highly paid, nor do they offer vast opportunities for promotion. Many are demanding, require a wide range of skills and involve long and irregular working hours. Some of the jobs entail working with handicapped, deprived, ill or difficult children. This can be emotionally demanding and often success is slow, slight or difficult to recognise.

But do not despair! The people we talked to all loved their work, had not been reduced to nervous wrecks, and intended to continue in the same job. It seems that if this kind of work is right for you, it is never boring, never humdrum and is always absorbing and worthwhile. It is also work where personality often counts more than qualifications on paper. Although educational attainments are never wasted, it is possible to work with children if, for some reason, you have not had success with exams. But you must be the right kind of person – have a good standard of spoken English, be calm and organised, warm and responsive to children and have plenty of imagination and common sense.

Although this book is written mainly for the school-leaver deciding on a career, many of the jobs are also ideal for older people with experience of life. So if you are looking for a change of career or, perhaps, thinking of embarking on one now that your own children have grown up, you may find something of interest here. Many of the training institutions waive their entry requirements for mature students, so lack of academic awards is not necessarily a disadvantage. If you embark on a course you will not find yourself alone among a crowd of 18-year-olds. Most courses have students of mixed ages and backgrounds and you will find that your own experience of life will help you with the work of the course.

Chapter 1
Working with Young Children

This chapter describes working with children in the first age group: from birth up to the age of five. The jobs will vary considerably. For instance, a playleader in a hospital will work in a very different atmosphere and be faced with a very different set of problems from the worker in a neighbourhood playgroup.

Despite these differences, one award is usually accepted as the qualification for all these jobs. This is the Council of Awards for Children's Care and Education (CACHE) qualification, the NNEB (Diploma of the National Nursery Examination Board). CACHE was formerly known as the NNEB; although the Council's name has changed, the qualification keeps the old name. The Scottish Nursery Nurses' Board makes an independent but similar award to students who have successfully completed a course of relevant SCOTVEC National Certificate modules.

There is another qualifying course which is favoured by some employers, especially the larger social services departments, as it involves employers in its running. This is the two-year course leading to the professional social work qualification, the Diploma in Social Work (DipSW). See page 99. The course is probably more appropriate for people working in an area of social stress than for playworkers or nursery assistants.

City and Guilds have also developed a child care scheme, 3240; Caring for Children (0–7 years). This popular scheme is aimed at mature carers of children (18+) either in post or for those who care for young children in a range of settings.

If, for any reason, you would like to start work as an untrained employee (perhaps in the hope that you will later be able to take some in-service training), there are some courses which, although they do not lead to qualifications, will prepare you for work.

The Pre-school Playgroups Association PPA runs part-time courses (see page 15) which are regarded as a useful preparation for work with young children, and there are two full-time courses which provide a general introduction to all aspects of community care. These are the CCETSW's Diploma in Social Work (DipSW) and the City and Guilds 3310: Family and Community Care, see pages 99 and 94. City and Guilds also provide a general certificate in care which can be obtained on a part-time, day-release basis.

National Vocational Qualifications in child care and education are awarded by BTEC or the Council for Early Years Awards; in playwork by City and Guilds.

Day Nurseries or Day Centres

Day nurseries are places where children who need care outside their own homes can spend the day. They are run by the social services departments of local authorities, by voluntary organisations, and sometimes privately. They accept children from babyhood and keep them until they are old enough to start full-time school. The children will be there for a variety of reasons: some will be children of single parents who have to go out to work; some will, as the expression is, have 'failed to thrive' because they have suffered some form of neglect; some will have come from such bad home situations that they are in danger of being abused if their parents are not given some form of relief.

The job of caring for these children obviously involves considerable emotional stress. When heavy demands are made on workers occasionally they fail to cope sympathetically with their task, but this is becoming less common as conditions and training improve. What we describe here is general policy on the running of day nurseries, and the attitudes we found are now fairly widespread.

Qualifications

Workers in day nurseries are called nursery officers. The qualification most generally required is the NNEB or SNNB Diploma. This is an area of work where untrained workers may be appointed as long as they have some suitable experience with children. Another form of training favoured by some employers is the college- or work-based version of the Diploma in Social Work which replaces the CSS. Both courses are widely available.

The Work

Day nurseries are usually open between 8 or 8.30 am and 6 pm, and remain open during school holidays as they cater primarily for children whose parents are unable to look after them because of ill health or social problems. Most day nurseries prefer to work with the whole family rather than just with the child. Some may, in fact, call themselves family centres. This means that parents are welcome to come to the centre whenever they wish, although this may often make the task of coping with the children more difficult.

It is necessary to win the co-operation of parents as the aim of the centre is to improve life for the children in their own family.

At the centre, the nursery officers should give the children loving attention, any physical care they may need (all day nurseries have a good supply of clean clothes) and a variety of interesting activities to occupy them. This last aspect is very important as one of the commonest forms of neglect is under-stimulation. A child who is left for long periods with nothing to do, who is ignored and not talked to, becomes passive and silent. A large number of such children are sent to day nurseries and they must be drawn into interesting activities if they are to develop normally.

The nursery officer will have complete responsibility for a group of children and be involved with their total day – feeding, toileting, washing and changing, as well as playing – and, while having a concern for them as individuals, will also have to manage them as a group. There will inevitably be conflicts, aggressions, jealousies and emotional demands to be sorted out. It is rather like having a large and difficult family, except that there is the comfort of supportive colleagues and of working in a team.

As places in day nurseries are few and far between, children are referred by social workers. This means that each child will have a social worker with whom the nursery officer must co-operate in sorting out any special problems. The nursery officer must also be capable of assessing a child's needs and of judging when a problem should be referred to another agency.

Qualities Required
The nursery officer must be a resilient all-rounder; calm and well-organised, understanding yet firm, warm and responsive with the children, but not so emotionally involved as to become bogged down by the sad situations some are in. Imagination and resourcefulness are needed to find activities which will gain the interest of even the most withdrawn child. An interest in music or art and crafts can be an advantage here. At the same time, the nursery officer must be capable of dealing with difficult parents who may undermine the caring work being done and who will also need help with their own problems. On top of this, the nursery officer must have the confidence to liaise with other professional colleagues, especially social workers, who may themselves be overworked and harassed. If you do not feel too daunted by all this, you will be a welcome worker in a difficult and demanding field which can also have its rewards.

Opportunities
Although there are no standardised rules for people employed outside the statutory sector, council-employed workers have a defined career structure. If you start at the bottom as an untrained

worker (not all authorities employ untrained people, however) you can take in-service training and become a nursery officer. The next grade is that of senior nursery officer and above that are the deputy organiser and organiser. The organiser is responsible for the whole centre and for setting the general policy and aims by which it is run. This is a post of considerable responsibility but one which can afford great job satisfaction.

Case Studies

Lesley, Nursery Officer in a Council Day Centre

I came into this job by accident really. I was out of work and a friend asked me if I would like to help out in the playgroup she ran. I went, thinking that it would be for a fortnight, and I stayed for two years.

While I was working in the playgroup I did both the PPA courses, which I found very helpful, and then I applied for my present job. I was employed here as an untrained assistant and have just finished doing my NNEB as in-service training. The best parts of the course for me were the discussion groups. They were a great relief from the constant contact with the children and gave me the opportunity to talk out the problems I have had to face in my work. It was also good to visit other nurseries and see how other people work. But I was disappointed that the course was not more helpful on behaviour problems. However much stimulation and play opportunity you offer, these do occur in the group situation of a day nursery.

I take the toddlers' group here. We have just organised them into age groups as we found that some children were missing out when we had all ages in together. We each have our own group so that we can form really close relationships with them.

Parents can be a problem sometimes, especially when their ways of dealing with their children are different from ours. Parents can come and go at any time and sometimes they stay, not to be with their children but to have a rest, enjoy a bit of company or to talk about their own problems. They are always welcome, but the children are often more difficult when their parents are here – especially if the child wants to be with the parent but the parent just wants to sit down quietly somewhere and rest. When this happens, we just cope as best we can because we consider the parents as much a part of the job as the children.

I think the parent is the most important person to the child and I'm uncertain how much responsibility we should take. We have one boy who is disliked by his mother. He is brought to us all day and put to bed immediately he gets home. Sometimes he spends 15 hours in bed. He has no relationship with his mother and she gives him no physical care either. We wash him and attend to him for his sake, because he needs it, but really his mother should be doing this. Although in cases like this we get help from social workers, it is very difficult to decide what is best.

Richard, Co-ordinator at a Voluntary Day Nursery

This nursery was started by a Quaker organisation eight years ago. It relies heavily upon council funding, and in return we take most of our children from the council's day centre list. We are accommodated in part of a church and do not have facilities for babies – our youngest children are aged two – but soon we will be moving into premises especially converted for us with money provided by the council.

There are both advantages and disadvantages in working outside the statutory sector. It is nice to feel you are working in an autonomous unit and not directed from above by a large bureaucracy with standardised systems and aims. And the fact that we have parents on our management committee means, I think, that they feel really involved in a way which is helpful. But funding can be a hassle. We have to renew our grant application each year and the money we get is subject to political changes in the town hall. In general, we can pay our workers on a par with council-employed nursery officers, but there is no guarantee of this when times are hard.

I joined the nursery three months after it opened. I had begun training as a teacher, but I was not temperamentally suited to the work. Maintaining discipline was a major drawback. So I gave it up and after a few years in temporary jobs, and feeling strongly that I wanted work to which I could feel committed, I applied for the post at this nursery.

I had no qualifications or relevant experience but I found that I had an immediate rapport with very young children. I was able to respond to them on an intuitive level. They require a lot of affection but they also respond readily, so you get a very quick feedback. I gained a great deal of fulfilment from it. But there were difficulties too. Young children make constant demands – for attention, diversion, comfort – and it took a while to adapt to this. Also, no one is a robot and there are days when you respond more easily than on others. But you relax into it and become accustomed to the noise! Some children are strongly affected by their home circumstances and they display it in the nursery, but on the whole there is little difference between our council-sponsored children and those who come to us privately. There's a lot of humour in young children and I enjoy this.

When we appoint staff, we do so only after we have invited candidates to visit us informally. We leave them for a while with the children and watch the way they respond to them. This is the important thing – as important as any formal qualifications or impressive experience.

Playgroups and Crèches

Playgroups and crèches cater for pre-school children and are usually non-profit-making community or church groups, or privately run. But there the similarity ends, because each has very separate aims, and responds to different needs.

The Playgroup

The growth of playgroups in the 1960s was due largely to the initiative taken by parents who realised the importance of social play for young children. The result was the setting up of the Preschool Playgroups Association (PPA) which is now a nationwide organisation. The head office is in London and there are separate sister organisations for Wales, Scotland and Northern Ireland (see Useful Addresses).

Most playgroups belong to the PPA because of the advantages this gives them and they adhere, more or less, to the ideals of the organisation. The movement is a child-orientated one and based very much on parental involvement. Although there are workers who run and co-ordinate the activities of each playgroup, most groups expect parents to help out on a rota basis. Generally, children are accepted in the term during which they are three and can stay in the group until they begin full-time school, but the local authorities may vary in their registration requirements. Children usually spend either the morning or the afternoon in the playgroup, rarely the whole day. Parents are charged a small fee which goes towards paying for equipment, materials, rent, running costs and wages.

The Playgroup Worker

As playgroups do not come under any statutory provision, most workers' salaries are paid out of fees and are fixed by management committees. There are no standard pay scales and pay can vary considerably from one area to another. In general, you can expect to be paid more in an area known to devote resources generously to matters of social concern, and less in places where social provision is minimal. The PPA would like the level of local authority funding and support to be similar throughout the country and is working to achieve this. In any event, you cannot expect a career structure as a playgroup worker, but the job itself can be very satisfying and is good experience for other kinds of work with children.

Playgroups are usually happy places. The worker manages the group and provides stimulating activities in very much the same way as the nursery assistant does. However, the playgroup worker has total responsibility for the day-to-day running of the group (there is nobody organising *you*) but in most cases is, of course, accountable to a management committee. There will usually be at least one parent helping out and this situation must be managed tactfully in a way which benefits both the parents and the children. Relationships between parents and playgroup workers often become very close, and workers may find themselves advising on general family matters. They must, indeed, be able to tackle a variety of tasks because they will also be responsible, often with the help of a committee of parents, for managing the money taken in fees and could be asked to organise fund-raising projects for such things as improvements to playgroup premises.

The central organisation of the PPA provides a firm structure of support for workers. At the top is the Head Office, and below this the regions, counties and branches, each with their own advisory staff. There are paid office and advisory staff at national and regional levels; some counties have county organisers who may or may not be paid; and many branches have area organisers who are mainly voluntary but receive expenses. Most branch committees arrange regular meetings for playgroup workers which can be very useful for exchanging ideas, discussing difficulties and generally making people feel that they are not working alone.

Playgroups are widespread in the British Isles and can be found in rural areas as well as in the larger cities. If you are interested in this kind of work, you should write to the PPA Head Office (address on page 111) to find out the name and address of your local county chairman or organiser, who will be able to give you information about the opportunities available where you live. Details of PPA training are given on page 93.

Case Studies

Betty and Maureen, Playgroup Workers

We both became involved through taking the PPA course. We had intended it as an opening to a nursery school job, but as it turned out, we stayed here.

This playgroup is housed in an Adult Education Institute, and at first there was great opposition to the idea of having children here at all. We started 10 years ago with six children, two tables and six chairs. Now we run sessions every morning and afternoon with about 20 children and, as you can see, we have plenty of equipment. We are also well integrated with the Institute and there are no problems in that direction.

We are a demonstration playgroup for the PPA courses held in the Institute. This means that our salaries are funded by the LEA, and that groups of students come to observe activities here to back up their course work. We don't get any further funding. All the equipment and materials are paid for out of the small charge we make to parents and donations from various sources. We are collecting for an extension hut at the moment.

The set-up of the playgroup is ideal for young children. It is somewhere for the child to play and be with other children, and it demands the involvement of the parent so that the child does not feel abandoned among strangers. We always have one or two parents helping on a rota basis each session, so children can see that someone's mum or dad is around. And when they are not helping in the playgroup, parents can attend classes at the Institute.

We both think that the feminist movement has done mothering a lot of damage – but that is just a personal opinion. Mothers now *expect* to have their children taken off their hands at the earliest age. We get people enquiring if we will take babies. We have to be strict about our admittance age: we take children only from the age of three. Before that they are too young to take part in the activities we offer, and to cope with the group situation.

We offer an alternative to nursery classes and we believe we have the edge on them because of the parental involvement. We find that this habit of involvement, started in the playgroup, continues as the child goes to school. Our parents often become the leading lights in the PTAs of the local schools. We also provide a more natural family atmosphere. The mums and dads who help often have babies and toddlers with them in the group. We work really closely with the parents and often find ourselves acting as unofficial marriage guidance counsellors and advisers on all sorts of matters!

Pam, Playgroup Worker

I've been running this playgroup for about seven years now. We are a member of PPA but we don't go along fully with all their ideas. I suppose I think them too idealistic today when so many mothers have to work to make ends meet. So we accept our children at the age of two-and-a-half and we run all-day playgroups. That is where we part company from PPA, but otherwise I think this playgroup is much like any other. We have a similar range of activities, and children get plenty of love and attention and all of them are happy. If any children were not happy here, I wouldn't keep them.

We run on a council grant which allows me to employ three full-time and two part-time helpers. We have mothers helping out when we are pushed, and if they need it we can usually afford to pay them a couple of pounds out of funds. I got my experience by helping at the playgroup my two kids attended. Then I got on to the committee, and when the playleader became ill I took over. Eventually, when my kids started school, I thought I could run a playgroup – and that's how I came to be here.

I was a nurse originally, and I think at first I tried to run this place as if it were a hospital ward. I wanted everything to be spotless and orderly. But I realised that kids need to run around and do messy activities and I became more informal. Even so, I like some structure and discipline. You can't wait until someone breaks a leg before telling them not to jump from the top of the climbing frame. They must learn that there are things that they can do and things that they can't.

I think that a lot of parents find it difficult to accept me because I'm black. When they first come they invariably push straight past me as I'm standing at the door, and go up to one of my white assistants to ask who is in charge. They are always very embarrassed when they realise their mistake! I have got used to this kind of prejudice now because it happens every day. Anyway, these things don't matter with the children and the parents never take their kids away – they know I do the job well and their kids are happy here. I am here because I love these kids. If I didn't, I would leave and go back to nursing.

Working in a Crèche

This is a very mixed field as crèches are provided by a number of authorities and private employers and are used by parents in different ways. The names they go under vary – many are called day nurseries – but whatever they are called, the function of a crèche is to provide care for pre-school children from babyhood, and free their parents to do something else. Crèches are found mainly in factories, hospitals, colleges, adult educational institutes and health centres.

The main functional difference between one crèche and another is the length of time the children are cared for. Crèches catering for the children of working parents take the children for the whole length of the working day, five days a week, whereas those in colleges and adult education institutes have the children only while the parent is actually studying on the premises. This may amount to much of the week or only a few hours here and there, and there may be considerable opportunity for the parent to visit the child and undertake some care during this time. Health centres usually take children on an irregular or part-time basis.

The length of time that the children stay affects the kind of care the crèche worker must give. If the hours of attendance are long you can expect to be responsible for total care, including feeding and changing. If the child is in the crèche for only a short time, such care may not be necessary.

Whatever the situation, the work is hard. Babies and young children need constant watching, and problems arise from having many of them together. Babies can swallow small objects, eat sand, or pull each other's hair. A newly mobile child does not realise the dangers of his activities either to himself or to floor-bound babies whose fingers he may step on. The list of possible hazards is endless and the workers must constantly foresee and prevent them.

For this age group more than for any other, the workers must make themselves into mother-substitutes; they must be able to respond lovingly to all the children in their care and give them the same amount of cuddling and physical contact that they should get from their parents.

Conditions of work vary greatly. Although every crèche is required to register with its local social service authority, which may choose to have some say in the staffing arrangements and accommodation, no minimum standards are laid down by law. Government recommendations are that there should be at least one staff member to every five children – more if the children are very young – but these may or may not be followed. There are, sadly, many crèches where facilities are poor and accommodation and equipment inadequate, but on the other hand there are good ones too, which are happy places for both the children and the staff.

Hours of work and holidays will vary. If you are caring for children during their parents' working day, you can expect the hours to be long and the holidays short. If you work in a college or adult education institute, the hours will probably be shorter and you may have the college holidays.

There is no central professional organisation for crèche workers and this means that no set salary scales have been negotiated. Usually, staff are fitted in somewhere in the salary structure of the institution to which they are attached – for instance, if you work in a hospital, you are likely to be paid on some grade of nurses' salary scales. But be warned, it is almost certainly going to be at the bottom end! Crèche workers have a lot of fighting to do if they are to receive fair recognition.

Qualifications

As there are no statutory qualifications for crèche workers, employers will set their own entry requirements. Often, a suitable personality and sympathy with the needs of young children will be enough to get you a job. Some experience with children, either your own or in a working situation, is always helpful, of course. Adult education institutes, which often have links with a PPA course, may require their workers to have taken it. Otherwise, the most appropriate form of training is the NNEB/SNNB Diploma.

Case Study

Valerie and Joy, Crèche Workers at an Adult Education Institute
This crèche takes only the children of students at the Institute. We take them up to the age of three, when they are old enough to go to the playgroup. The youngest we have is four months and we do get quite a few babies. Our insurance policy states that the parent must be on the premises and this means that our numbers vary from day to day according to who has classes. On a busy day we can have 16 children, but it can drop to half a dozen or less. The children are only away from their parents for two or three hours at a time and mostly they seem to really enjoy it.

We've both been here for two years. The Institute wanted people who had done the PPA course, which we both had. One of us also had previous experience in playgroups. Although the pay is bad, and no one has got around to giving us a rise since the local education authority took over our financing 18 months ago, we like the work. And we live nearby, so it's convenient. We work from 9.30 am until 4 pm and get the Institute holidays, but as we are paid on an hourly basis we don't get holiday pay. The summer holiday is 12 weeks, so you certainly miss the money. We have done summer playscheme work to earn a bit. Also, it's nice to be with the older children for a change.

On the whole, the children here are very good. We do have some screamers, but if they get too upset we fetch their mothers to deal with them. In two years we've only had two children who haven't settled. The babies are easy because they don't notice the difference, and if they grow up with us they are used to us by the time they are toddlers. The most difficult children to settle are those between one and two years who have never been away from their mothers before.

When we get a new child, we explain to the mother what the rules are. We don't change the children or give them their lunch. The mother must do that. We need our lunch break, although it's only half an hour. We then ask the mother what the child is used to – whether it has a bottle or a dummy and what routine she uses for getting it to take a rest. We try to do exactly what she does. We've even carried babies on our backs in slings!

The children need watching continuously – there are so many dangers when they're very young. So the work is tiring, both physically and mentally. As we've only got one room, we choose activities to fit in with the children who are here. If we have a lot of babies we don't do painting, as it can so easily get out of control. Also, our slide, which the older ones love, can be too much of a hazard when a lot of the very young ones are here. But dough is popular with all ages and we use it a lot.

We've heard from some people that we are very lucky here. We are well equipped and have our own room. Apparently, some people have to work in the canteen or tucked away in any odd corner – and often with almost no equipment. That must be very difficult.

Nursery and Infant Schools

Local education authorities run nursery schools and nursery classes in infant schools. The number to be found differs widely from one part of the country to another. In general, the large cities provide a high number of nursery places and the country areas, with one or two notable exceptions, very few.

Nursery education caters for three- and four-year-olds and takes place during normal school hours. Children may attend for all, or part, of the day. Half-day attendance is most usual. It is not a child-minding service – the hours are not long enough to be useful to the working mother – nor is it linked to social need. It is inspired by the belief that the pre-school years are ones of intense capacity for learning and developing. It aims to encourage the emotional, social and intellectual development of the children and to prepare them for full-time school.

The Nursery Assistant

In charge of each nursery class is a teacher who has a teaching qualification, and a nursery assistant who, usually, has an NNEB (in Scotland an SNNB) Diploma. The nursery assistant works under the supervision of the teacher and the exact balance of work is a matter for the two people to decide. There will be some statutory obligations and responsibilities set down by the local education authority, such as hours of work and arrangements for sick children, and there is usually an understanding that the assistant will take on most of the practical work such as clearing up and supervision of toileting arrangements. Beyond this, most assistants can expect to be fully involved with the activities of the class and to work in partnership with the teacher. There is, of course, always the possibility that an individual teacher may wish to keep her assistant in a subservient role, but this attitude is not commonly found these days.

The nursery class is organised on informal lines and offers a range of activities such as singing, listening to stories, music-making, painting and craft work, some simple cooking and plenty of play opportunities. Learning in the formal sense is not attempted, but basic number and reading skills are introduced informally through the activities.

The children using nursery classes are likely to be a normal mix, needing the usual amount of love and reassurance but seldom having any particular emotional difficulties. The emphasis, therefore, is on providing activities and giving suitable help with them. There are not likely to be any special discipline problems, though any lively bunch of three- and four-year-olds will need calm, common-sense organisation and supervision.

Qualities Required

If you enjoy being with young children, are reasonably calm and practical, and can 'let your hair down' in the telling of stories and singing of songs, you may be cut out to be a nursery assistant. You must be responsive to the chatter and achievements of young children and be imaginative and able to develop activities with them. An ability in music, art or crafts is an advantage and you must have good spoken English, as language is very important in the development of the young child. Finally, you must remember that behind each child are the parents, who may be anxious about their child's first excursion into the big world outside and who may need your sympathetic reassurance and advice.

Training

Authorities prefer to recruit trained staff, so the first step towards a job as a nursery assistant is to go to college and take your NNEB or SNNB Diploma. Some large authorities run sponsorship schemes whereby suitable people are recruited untrained and then sent to college to take a qualifying course. This has the advantage of providing you with a salary during your training and assuring you of a job at the end of it. But you may well find that the scheme is limited to people with real financial need, such as single parents or older people with financial responsibilities. If you think you may be eligible for a sponsorship, you should apply to the staffing section of your local education office to see if your authority runs a scheme.

Opportunities and Prospects

If you live in a rural area you will, unfortunately, have little opportunity for nursery school work. In large cities the openings are usually good and the best initial contact is through your work experience during your NNEB course. Many jobs are filled through personal contact made in this way. Otherwise, jobs are advertised in the local press, the professional journal of the LEA (to be found in staff rooms or through the head teacher) and occasionally in *The Times Educational Supplement*. Once appointed, you will be in a secure pensionable job which, although not offering any promotion within that field, should provide good experience should you wish to transfer to another area of work with children. For those with family responsibilities, the advantages of the short working day and the school holidays are invaluable and may make the difference between being able to work and having to remain at home.

Case Study

Jackie (21), Nursery Assistant

I really do enjoy my job. When I left school, I worked for a year in an office. I wouldn't have missed it because I learnt what I *didn't* want to do. Office work made me very fed up and bored. I've worked in this nursery class for just over a year, and before I went to college to do my NNEB I worked in a private day nursery for a year and a half. There are many similarities, except that in the day nursery I did shift work and the children had more emotional needs, became more emotionally dependent on you as they were away from their parents for long periods. Here, they need love and attention too, but mostly they come for the activities we provide and to prepare for full-time school.

I work with one nursery teacher and we work very much as a team, both of us preparing and then helping with the activities. She knows more about the number and pre-reading work than I do and organises most of the material for this kind of work herself, and I am the one who deals with the more practical matters – teaching the children to dress themselves and to know about personal hygiene. I check that they have washed their hands after going to the toilet and make sure they know why they should do this, but otherwise we share the work, concentrating on the things we enjoy or do well. For instance, I think she is better at telling stories than I am, but I like singing songs with the children and helping them to join in with the actions. We both do observations on children if we suspect they may have any special problems.

I think it is really important to have a good relationship with the parents. If the children can see you getting on well with them it gives them a feeling of security, especially if at any time there is a family upheaval. It also makes discussion easier if any problems do crop up. It can be very hard to tell parents that their child ought, for instance, to see a speech therapist if you have not already established easy contact.

I want to stay working with children. It's never boring and sometimes one comment can last you for months! I should like to have a go at everything – day nursery, child minding, even short-term fostering. But at the moment I'm happy where I am.

Infant Schools

In infant schools, where the needs of very young children are met, it is common for the teachers to have some extra assistance. This is especially necessary in areas where there is little nursery provision and children are admitted to school at the age of four plus, and in inner city areas where social stress makes the task of the infant teacher more difficult. This help is provided in the form of auxiliary assistants (sometimes called ancillary, or school, assistants).

The Auxiliary Assistant

Auxiliaries need not be qualified, though there is an increasing tendency to employ people with an NNEB Diploma if they are available. They must, however, have some experience with children and a sensible and sympathetic attitude to them is always required. Some authorities offer on-the-job training at teachers' centres for unqualified workers.

The auxiliary assistant is directly responsible to the head teacher and unlike the nursery assistant does not work in partnership with any one teacher. Because of the slightly more formal attitude to learning in the infants' class, the auxiliary will rarely be involved in helping with classroom activities, but will be engaged mainly on practical matters. Responsibilities commonly include maintenance and preparation of equipment, supervision of children outside the classroom – in the playground, at lunch, at the toilets – and helping with dressing and undressing for PE. Many schools rely on the help of auxiliaries on school outings and in cases such as illness or school phobia when a particular child needs individual attention.

Most auxiliary assistants' posts are obtained by personal contact or word of mouth. Sometimes advertisements are placed in the local press. The job is secure and pensionable and, with a short working day and school holidays, fits in very well with family life.

Working in a Hospital

There are two types of non-medical work with children in hospitals. They are very different from each other and have in common only the hospital setting. Nursery nurses are employed on maternity wards and in special care units to look after the day-to-day needs of new-born babies, and play specialists are employed on children's wards to cater for the play needs of young patients.

If you are interested in either kind of work, you must remember that hospitals are run on formal lines. Tasks are very clearly defined and there is a strictly observed hierarchy of accountability among staff. You will certainly wear a uniform and be addressed as 'nurse' if you work on a maternity ward. This will probably not be the case if you work as a play specialist. In any event, you must be prepared to accept hospital discipline as part of the job.

Maternity Wards

In maternity wards, nursery nurses have certain specific responsibilities for the babies. Most hospitals accept people with an NNEB/ SNNB qualification and give further in-service training.

A nursery nurse does much more than cuddle, bathe and dress doll-like new-born babies. She has responsibility for the nursery where the babies are cared for, and must see that rigorous standards of hygiene are maintained to reduce the chance of cross-infection. She sees that clean nappies, towels and bed linen are available and that a cot is always ready for the next newcomer. She is also responsible for observing, weighing and checking the babies to make sure they are all well and thriving and must alert the medical staff if she suspects all is not well. She will also have to look after the milk and equipment used for bottle feeding and may be asked to assist with light domestic tasks such as cleaning cots and lockers before a new patient uses them.

Another important part of the job is educating the mother in baby care. Many first-time mothers need a lot of help and the nursery nurse is on hand to assist them. She will give the baby a demonstration bath, explain how to change nappies, prevent nappy rash and get the baby's wind up after feeding. Whether the mother is breast or bottle feeding, she can expect help and advice from the nursery nurse. She will need sympathy and reassurance too. After eight days she will be at home, alone with her baby, and the time spent in hospital can give her the confidence and knowledge she needs.

The nursery nurse's educating role is not confined to working with the mothers. Student nurses must also learn baby care and this is demonstrated by the nursery nurse.

On the medical side, the nursery nurse must arrange for each baby to have certain tests at the appropriate time, and may also be required to assist with some routine medical treatments. If she wishes, she may, after further training, work in the special care or premature baby unit. Some hospitals train their own nursery nurses for this work; some require the nurse to take a neonatal paediatric course.

Qualities Required

Because hygiene is so important in the care of new-born babies, the nursery nurse should be scrupulously clean and tidy both in her person and in the way she works. No new mother will want a nurse with dirty fingernails or unwashed, untidy hair to handle her baby. Nor will she want her baby to be in a nursery which is not neat, clean and methodically arranged. The nursery nurse must be able to boost confidence, and herself have the confidence to fulfil her teaching role.

As a nursery nurse, you will be one of the nursing team. You will be directly accountable to the midwife or ward sister, and must be prepared for shift work which will include night duty. If your job takes you away from home, you will have the opportunity of living in the hospital nurses' home.

Finding a Job

Although nursery nurses are employed on maternity wards throughout the British Isles, there are some country areas where jobs cannot be found, as there are enough midwives available to carry out the baby care work. This is almost never the case in urban areas. Many hospitals do not need to advertise jobs, as they take part in the work experience schemes of local colleges and obtain staff through personal knowledge of students. When jobs are advertised, the local papers, the *Nursing Times* and *Nursery World* are the most usual media used. As advertisements appear infrequently, it is quite in order for you to write directly to individual hospitals to ask if they have a vacancy.

Case Study

Jane (19)

While I was training, some people would say 'only nursery nursing?' when they asked what course I was taking. People don't seem to realise what is involved. At the end of the day at work I am absolutely exhausted.

I might not have known about nursery nursing if it hadn't been for the careers adviser at school. I had always wanted to nurse, ever since I was a little girl, but when we began to do dissection in biology all the blood rather put me off! I explained this to the careers adviser when I was in the fifth year, and when she heard that I was fond of children and had been taking a young children's Sunday school class since I was 13½, she suggested that I should take an NNEB.

I did the course at an individual Nursery Training Centre in the town near my home after I had taken my O levels. I took English, biology, music and geography at O level and I found them all useful for the course, especially the English. It is so important to be able to take notes and summarise information.

During the course I did work practice in a number of settings, and during my second year I did a three-week block practice in a maternity hospital. I loved it and that decided me to try for hospital work. I wrote away to 10 hospitals and this one was the first to offer me an interview – and I got the job.

I haven't regretted it. It is so rewarding. Many of the first-time mums are very nervous and unsure, and it is part of my job to help them gain confidence. I help them with feeding, bathing and changing their babies and I'm on hand if they have any special problems. Because I am concerned specifically with the babies, I am usually the person the mums come to with their worries. If you have done your job well you can see a tremendous improvement, so that by the time a mum goes home she is coping well with her baby.

I am also responsible for the day-to-day care of the baby – seeing that it is gaining weight as it should, that the cord is clean and dry, and that standards of hygiene are maintained. If I am not happy about anything I refer the problem to the midwife so that the baby can have medical attention. It is quite a responsibility. I also arrange that babies have tests on the appropriate day, but I cannot give these tests myself because the NNEB course does not include anatomy and some of these tests involve pricking the heel. I think the NNEB ought to cover the necessary information so that the nursery nurse could be qualified for certain basic medical routines.

I have been working here for six months now. It was a bit of a surprise at first to be called 'nurse' and to find myself demonstrating baby care to student nurses, but it soon becomes part of the job. I live in the nurses' home which is very pleasant and makes me feel part of the hospital community.

The Play Specialist

Going into hospital can be an ordeal for children. They may find themselves away from home for the first time and they will almost certainly have to submit to medical treatments which may be frightening and painful. Hospitals now recognise this and employ play specialists on their children's wards to care for the emotional well-being of these young patients. A hospital play specialist works with children aged from 0 to 16 years. As well as being ill, they may have disabilities; some children will be immobilised, on bed rest or be in isolation. Others will be terminally ill.

On the face of it, the play specialist organises play activities in the children's ward, both in the playroom and at the bedsides of children who cannot be moved. But really, the job goes far deeper than this. Play can be important in helping children to accept being in hospital. It should not merely divert attention from what is happening, but be used to enable children to understand their illness and accept with the minimum amount of fear the treatment they will have to undergo. Play specialists help to prepare children for their operations and treatments, helping to explain through play what will happen to them. They may, when a parent is unavailable, support a child during a treatment. Preparation is done through conversation, reading stories about hospital, and allowing children to dress up in nurses' and doctors' clothing and handle equipment. The play specialist gives every opportunity that is needed for acting out all aspects of hospital life.

While the hospital becomes a major play element, it is also important to maintain home links. Again, conversation is important and homely activities such as cooking are helpful. A good relationship between the play specialist and the sick child's parents is equally essential. The hospitalisation of a child can cause parents great anxiety; they too may feel ill at ease in the hospital atmosphere. It is the play specialist who can most easily encourage parents to take a full part in their child's life in hospital, explaining ways in which they can help both the child and the medical staff.

In some specialist hospitals, play can be used to help children regain manual skills they have lost in the course of their illness and medical treatment. This entails a high degree of co-operation between the play specialist and the medical team. But even where this is not the case, some basic knowledge of medical procedures and the illnesses of the children in the ward is needed. The play specialist should know, for instance, which children are on special diets or cannot eat or drink because they are awaiting their operations. It is best when the play specialist works as one of the team with the medical staff, attends report at the changeover of shifts and is generally seen to take part in the whole life of the hospital, not just in the nice play and fun aspects. This kind of total involvement is the best way of gaining the confidence of the children and their parents.

Qualities Required
You need considerable maturity to do this work and you must have had experience of working with normal, healthy children and must really want to do hospital work. Television serials tend to glamorise hospital life, but really it isn't like that. There is a lot of hard work and stress and the play specialist may well have to fight for recognition within the medical team. You must be able to prove your worth by showing that you understand how children can react to hospitalisation, which may make them regress, and by demonstrating what play can do to help their recovery. You will also have to take your share of work rounds, attending meetings and writing notes, and you should have the confidence and ability to express your opinions. You must be flexible, as it is usually not possible to programme the activities in the playroom, and you must respond to a situation which is changing each day as children come and go with their different illnesses.

Training
Hospital play specialists are required to hold the Hospital Play Specialist Certificate, or be prepared to take this training. Occasionally, a second qualification such as nursing or teaching is required. For information on courses for hospital play specialists see page 106.

Opportunities
The DHSS report, *Play for Children in Hospital*, was published in 1976. This recommended that hospitals employ play specialists, but it was not until 1990 with the publishing of the document *Quality Management of Children: Play in Hospital* (PHLC) that all hospitals began to look seriously at qualifications for play staff and

appropriate remuneration. It is now fully recognised that the job of a play specialist is a full-time one and that it is unsatisfactory and confusing for the children if play staff are involved in nursing duties. In general, if the paediatrician is fully appreciative of the contribution a play specialist can make, the job will be rewarding and the other medical staff will follow his or her lead.

Salary scales for play specialists are currently under discussion and more and more hospitals are using a salary scale of their own for play staff. Information about work as a play specialist can be obtained from Save the Children Fund and from the National Association for the Welfare of Children in Hospital (NAWCH). Please send a large sae and expect a small charge for information.

Case Study

Fiona, Play Specialist in a Large Children's Hospital

I work on a ward taking children with neurological disorders and, broadly speaking, my job is to make their stay in hospital more enjoyable by providing play opportunities. On this ward I also have the task of helping them, through play, to re-acquire manual skills they may have lost in the course of their illness and medical treatment.

In order to help them I treat each child individually, as each illness is different and activities suitable for one child may be inappropriate for another. Sometimes they cannot concentrate for long, and this is another reason why I cannot set up any one main activity in the playroom. So I try to organise suitable kinds of individual play. Sometimes this involves a lot of improvisation. For instance, after spinal operations children must lie on their front or side, so I have to find an activity which they can do in this position. Dexterity play is important to help the movement in hands and limbs. Recently, a four-and-a-half year old came in with a brain tumour. She was very bright and a beautiful painter. After her operation she lost a lot of mobility in her hands and she had to start all over again using her left hand. This was a frightening experience, and I tried to help her understand what had happened as well as re-learn the skills she had lost.

I find it is an advantage not being part of the medical staff. I don't wear a uniform and this enables me to be a real friend and comfort to those children for whom a white coat or starched dress represents fear and is, more often than not, associated with pain. I also play the innocent with parents so that they can tell me what is the matter with their child. This can help them at an emotionally distressing time.

The benefits of bringing as much pleasure and fun as possible to sick children make this by far the most satisfying job I have done. To distract the children from their confusion and discomfort by providing them with books, toys and creative activities gives enormous pleasure to me as well as them. But I do have to keep an emotional distance, because many of our children are very ill indeed and I couldn't continue to do the job well if I became overwhelmed by the sadness of individual cases.

Private Posts

In days gone by, uniformed nannies were a common sight but today, outside the confines of Kensington Gardens, they are not much in evidence. In fact, there are more nannies around than you might imagine, but you may not always recognise a modern nanny when you see her. A few still work for rich or working parents, but most are likely to be employed by busy professional mums. There is plenty of opportunity for working with a private family in one of three types of job. You can be a daily, a resident or a temporary nanny.

Many working mothers need a nanny to take their place during the day when they are away, but will take over themselves when they return home. They will employ somebody on a daily basis, who will work set hours and return to her own home each evening. If they need more complete care for their children, or perhaps live in a country area, they may decide to employ a resident nanny, and in this case they must provide adequate private living accommodation for her - gone are the days when nannies were expected to sleep in the night nursery along with their charges! The third kind of employment is with families which need help to tide them over a difficult period, such as the birth of another child, the illness of the mother, or a parent's absence from home. This work may be residential or non-residential.

The Work of the Nanny

A nanny should look after the children of the family in an informal way, much as the mother would. She must, of course, follow the parents' wishes in the way she works, so it is sensible to make sure that you feel at home in the family atmosphere when you apply for a job. You will be responsible for feeding, changing, and playing with your charges and you will also take them on outings and deliver the older ones to school. You may also be required to take care of the children's clothes and their rooms but, apart from that, you should not be expected to do any domestic work. If you are a resident nanny, you can expect to be 'on call' during the evening and attend to the late feed of a young baby. But such demands should not be made to an unreasonable extent. Resident and day nannies who are employed by working mums and who spend the whole day alone with their charges may suffer the same feelings of loneliness and isolation that sometimes afflict young housebound mothers.

Qualities Required

Most employers will require you to have NNEB/SNNB or private college training or considerable experience, with good references. Beyond this you must be completely reliable and trustworthy, as you will be playing an important role in the private life of the family you work for. Tact and consideration are important, too, as you will have to fit in with the pattern of life of the household.

You must, of course, be competent to perform your specialist duties, that is, have a good knowledge of the development of young children and of the ways in which it can be encouraged. You will be coping with a variety of situations, so common sense and adaptability, and probably a sense of humour, will be helpful and you will need to be capable in practical ways. Cleanliness and safety too are both important when dealing with young children. Finally, you should be polite and have a pleasant manner of speaking as the children will learn from your example.

Conditions of work are essentially a matter to be arranged between you and your employer, but the National Association of Nursery Nurses has laid down some guidelines for nursery nurses seeking employment in private posts which you should find helpful. They recommend that you should not be required to undertake domestic duties beyond the care of the children and their nurseries and that extra responsibility should entitle you to extra pay. So if you find yourself left in sole charge, coping with a sick child or a very large family, or helping out with more work at a time of family crisis, you should be able to expect some more money for your efforts. This may sound rather mercenary, but it is a good insurance against being 'put upon', which can quite easily happen in private posts.

The Association also suggests fair rates of pay which will, of course, change from time to time, and states that you should have one regular day (24 hours) off each week. If you work on a day basis your day's work should not exceed eight hours, and if you are in a residential post you should be free of duties, except for baby feeds, after 7 pm. Your annual paid holiday should be four weeks and you should have all public holidays or days off in lieu. The Contracts of Employment Act stipulates that your employer must provide you with a written statement setting out particulars of the terms of your employment. Be sure to obtain this before you accept a private post.

Finding a Job

There are two main ways of finding a private post: first through advertisements which can be found in *The Lady* and *Nursery World*; second, through agencies which specialise in placing people in posts as nannies. It will not cost you anything to go on the books of an agency, as the cost of the service is borne by the employer. Most temporary jobs are found through agencies, though some people may advertise privately. Often, nannies move on to friends of the family – word of mouth can play an important role.

Those with appropriate training should have no difficulty in finding a job: the private colleges, which traditionally have trained girls for positions as nannies, do not turn out nearly enough students to meet the demand.

Most jobs are in the home counties or abroad. The further away from London you get, the fewer the opportunities for working as a nanny. If you would like to work abroad there are opportunities, particularly in the USA, the Middle East, South Africa and, sometimes, Australia.

Case Study

Erica, Nanny

This is my first job and I have been here over two years now. I look after two children aged two and five. Their mother does not work and we get on very well together so this is a great factor in making the job enjoyable. I am never alone with the children in the house for long periods and I like this because I am a sociable person. I think that some nannies can feel very lonely and isolated.

When I started here, the elder child was three and the baby was due in one month. When he was born, his mother breastfed him during the day but he slept in my room and I gave him night bottle feeds. He was an adorable baby, very easy and happy, and I have become very attached to him. The family had not previously had a nanny and the little girl was used to being with her mother so I had to get to know her - at a time which also coincided with the arrival of the baby. Fortunately there were no problems. She wasn't jealous of the baby - in fact, if anything she was over-helpful.

I soon found that the little girl enjoyed cooking, painting and other creative activities which she hadn't previously had the opportunity to do, so I do a lot of this with her. I also take her skating and swimming. I think this is one of the great advantages of having a nanny. As I am not responsible for any of the domestic work, I have plenty of time to introduce the children to a variety of activities.

I don't work to any rigid rules. It is a very give-and-take situation and the sharing of tasks has sorted itself out as we have gone along. I get the children up in the morning and sometimes drive the little girl to school. The rest of the day is mine and I decide what I will do with the children. Their mother cooks lunch and I do teas and puddings. I usually do the ironing but I am not expected to do any cleaning. I live as one of the family and eat with them.

I went to Norland College which is a private college, traditionally geared towards training students for private posts. The course is very full, and at the end students have three qualifications: the NNEB, the RSH (Royal Society of Health) and the Norland Diploma. We had a wide experience of work situations and were in constant contact with the children in the college nursery groups. Working for the RSH involved three months in a hospital, and to get the Norland Diploma we had to work satisfactorily with a family for nine months.

I began my training with the idea of getting a travelling job on board a liner, but I soon found out that those jobs are very hard to get and not as glamorous as they sound. I would still like to travel, but I don't think

I will do it in that way. I like working with a family because I enjoy the closeness I have with the two children. I realise I have been fortunate in finding this family, so I will almost certainly stay here a while longer.

Travelling Jobs

Opportunities for regular employment in this apparently desirable field are very few and far between. The major shipping companies employ a few nursery nurses on their cruise ships, mainly to provide play and crèche facilities for very young children, but they always have a waiting list. Naturally they can afford to be choosy, and they insist on an NNEB qualification or the equivalent and they prefer some job experience. They set a minimum age for employment which varies between 21 and 24, and claim that their jobs are so attractive that people stay in them for years. One company told us of a nursery nurse who had been with them for 25 years!

If you wish to try your luck, you should apply direct to the fleet personnel department of the shipping line. You can find the names and addresses of cruise operators in the travel pages of national newspapers or from your local travel agent. But be prepared to wait for your job.

Other opportunities for travelling work exist in the holiday sphere. This work entails dealing with older children, and details of it are given in Chapter 3.

Chapter 2

Residential Work

Residential work is to be found in establishments where the children actually live on the premises. Staff are not necessarily required to live in, but the children must be cared for around the clock and therefore work is arranged in shifts. As a resident worker, you would be expected to spend a minimum of two nights a week sleeping in.

There are two main types of residential establishment: children's homes, which cater for children who for one reason or another have been taken into care; and homes for children with a range of disabilities, a few of which may also provide their education. Some are run by local authorities through their social services or education departments; others by voluntary bodies such as the National Children's Home and Barnardo's.

Children's Homes

Children are taken into care for a variety of reasons: delinquency, drug abuse, illness of parents, abuse, neglect or rejection by parents, being beyond parental control; few are orphans. As things have to go very wrong indeed before children are taken from family into public care, the children have usually had a very bad time and often exhibit severe behavioural problems. Two-thirds of the children in care today are teenagers and many have been away from their families for some years. Many have been cared for in foster homes, but have failed to fit in with the foster families. In the home, the children lead as normal a life as possible, attending local schools, going out with their friends and pursuing their own interests. Homes are usually kept small – up to ten children – or, if large, are broken up into a number of smaller living units. There is a tendency to separate teenagers from other age groups because of the particular problems they pose, but categorising is kept to a minimum.

Most homes offer 'shorter stays', preparing children for fostering or for a return to their own homes. Many homes offer short-term care to give parents a break.

Working as a Residential Social Worker

Apart from domestic staff, people who work in children's homes look after the general welfare of the children and are called residential social workers. There are a few very young children in care; they are usually the easiest to place in foster homes so very few indeed end up in residential establishments. A residential social worker is much more likely to spend most of the time dealing with difficult and confused adolescents.

People's ideas on how homes should be run vary enormously. Some are run on authoritarian lines, in the belief that the children need firm discipline. Staff working in these establishments are expected to uphold the house rules and make discipline a major part of their job. Most homes, however, are organised more informally.

If you work in a home which aims to make its children independent, because they will soon have to go out into the world, you would expect your physical caring to be limited. Children must learn to cope with laundry and keep their own place tidy. They must also be able to prepare some food for themselves. On the other hand, you may find yourself much involved in counselling, attempting through conversation to make a child more self-aware and, perhaps, self-critical and thus more disposed to behave in a way that is socially acceptable. It also aims to make the person happier with himself or herself and better able to make decisions in a sensible manner.

Other homes set out to create a caring, family atmosphere. Here, the emphasis is upon the well-being of the group and although the problems of an individual member do, of course, receive attention, there is little formal counselling. Physical tasks will probably take up more time, as a certain amount of domestic work is inseparable from this kind of caring – home-made cakes, for instance, add a homely touch.

Whichever kind of home you work in, there are certain tasks you can expect to do. Behaviour must be kept within acceptable limits; leisure time must be, however loosely, organised; and contact must be maintained with each child's school. It is you, the residential social worker, who will go to the open evening or to see a child in the school play. You will organise the Bank Holiday outing and see that birthdays are remembered.

It must be stressed that the work of a residential social worker is demanding, the hours long and the rewards often difficult to identify. You may think that you have made great progress with a particular child, and then he or she may suddenly do something which seems to put you both back to square one. Or you may work long and hard with somebody seemingly without any effect. For this reason, most children's homes have some kind of support system for staff. There will be a visiting psychiatrist to give advice about problems with individual children, and someone similar with whom you can discuss your own personal problems if you wish. Voluntary organisations usually back up their workers.

Qualities Required

To be a residential social worker, you do not need impressive academic qualifications but you must be mature. You must be able to work well in a team, as supportive working relationships can ease the burden of the work, and you must really want to do this kind of work. You must like children and have the determination to succeed with them, have plenty of common sense and be able to take decisions on your own. Finally, you must be relaxed, even in difficult situations. Allowing tension to build up is the surest way of failing in this kind of work.

Training

Most young people entering their first job have no training specifically for residential work. They are selected for the personal qualities they seem to possess. They are usually required to have had some experience with children and are seldom accepted straight from school. The usual minimum age for a residential social worker is 21. If you leave school at 16, a Preliminary Course in Social Care is a good preparation for residential work. Otherwise, work with children on a voluntary basis is acceptable. Once you are in employment, you are likely to be given the opportunity to take in-service training.

Case Studies

Jenny (22), Residential Social Worker in a Council Children's Home Catering for Adolescents

I studied English at university, and during this time I worked in Women's Aid - a voluntary group offering support and alternatives to battered women and their children. I took this job in an adolescent community home to gain a year's experience before doing a course to qualify me for community work. I was initially looking for work with voluntary organisations but at the time grants for these jobs were not being renewed. I have now been here for over a year and it seems likely that I will be staying for a few months longer. The home is going through a period of great change as a new superintendent has been appointed and I want to be part of putting into practice the ideas we have been discussing. It is a chance to be in at the beginning of something and see it slowly build up. There is also the fact that it has taken this long to build up quite deep relationships with some of the kids, and I want to continue working with them for a while.

I found the job hard at first. We worked as a collective in Women's Aid and it was hard to adjust to the hierarchical structure of social services, though I'm lucky to be working in an establishment which is run on democratic principles. Also, after being in a small Northern town, it was something of a culture shock to be working in an inner city area with all its accompanying problems. The work is very intense – working with difficult, often quite disturbed adolescents – and one is constantly questioning one's judgement and attitudes to situations that crop up.

Working in a children's home is very much more than just physically catering for kids, which is something people outside the work often don't seem to realise. There are the old, preconceived ideas of the traditional residential social workers fulfilling a parental role. The caring aspect is obviously important, but residential social work means much more than that. It means dealing with kids who are non-school attenders, glue-sniffers, or those classified as delinquents. It means working closely with social workers, families, schools and psychologists. Also, it means helping kids find jobs and set up on their own. The job increasingly means looking beyond the work you do in the confines of the home. With present government policy leading to cuts in services you have to look at the implications this has on kids in care and try to preserve a situation where you can do the job satisfactorily.

Since I've been in this job eight staff have left, so that after little more than a year I'm one of the 'old' staff. Many people are like me – using the job as a means of getting into a related career, rather than looking at it as a career in itself. It is a stepping stone for many young people who haven't yet decided what to do. This is inevitable in a job where the opportunities for training are not always there, the pay is not that good, and demands on workers are great and the hours long and unsocial. The continual change of staff is obviously very frustrating for both kids and workers, and there has to be a very strong staff group to ensure that there is a continuity of ideas.

I like working with kids and I've enjoyed my time here, but I feel that I will still pursue a training which will qualify me to work with them more informally than in a residential setting.

Steve and Jane, Superintendent and Residential Social Worker in a Voluntary Organisation Children's Home

Steve: Work in children's homes is more difficult to get into nowadays. You don't need to be academic but you do need sensitivity – to be aware of yourself and the needs of others, to be relaxed, have patience and to be mature, though not necessarily in years.

We have five staff here looking after 11 children – three women and two men – and our ages range from 18 to 40. The mixture is good as we can all make our own, slightly different contribution. I need another man to provide a masculine presence when I'm away from the house.

One of the most important aspects of this work is that the staff should help each other. We don't have an official staff meeting, but we get together informally, at least once a week, usually around the kitchen table with a cup of tea. At these times we talk about our own problems as well as those of the children. It's vital that every member of staff knows I care about them as a person. We're a warm and caring bunch of people

– for each other and for the children. We aim at the warmth and security of a family. I must be acutely aware of the needs of the staff so that I can deal with every situation as it arises. In this way I can, I hope, prevent resentment and anxiety building up.

We don't have a set duty rota. We work out one each week and keep it as flexible as possible to suit each person's needs.

Jane: But the hours are long. We have two days off duty each week and we have two staff sleeping in each night. Sometimes it is not possible to give staff any other free evenings. This isn't much for a young person who wants to get out and meet friends.

Before coming into residential work, we did fostering for six years. Most of the children here come from foster homes where the situation has broken down. I think this is because the fostering situation is more difficult. You can cope with things here when you couldn't in your own home. The children are here for all sorts of reasons – neglect, cruelty, battering, rejection and being beyond their parents' control. You have to realise that they don't want to be here, don't think the staff are wonderful and don't love you more than they love their own parents. However bad the home has been, the parents are almost always the most important people.

Steve: We can accept this now – we can give a lot of ourselves without needing return. But it takes time. Young staff do need a response at first, to fuel them for the job, as it were.

I talk to the children about their parents. I haven't had a child in my care who wouldn't prefer to go home if the situation were happier. Often, children arrive with fears resulting from tales they have heard about life in care and these must be dispelled. A happy atmosphere must meet them at the door.

Residential Schools and Homes for Handicapped Children

Residential care is commonly available for children with three main kinds of disability: physical, mental and emotional. It is seldom possible to care for a mixed bunch of such children under the same roof, as different forms of disability demand quite different treatment. Also, it may not be easy for the children themselves to live together. For instance, a mobile, mentally retarded child can be a great danger in a group of physically handicapped children. His strength will be far greater than his understanding, and he can easily injure or run down children who are unable to get out of his way. So, although under present government policy more and more handicapped people are being integrated into the community, separate provision is still the rule in the residential establishments that still exist.

Care is provided by education authorities, local social services departments and voluntary organisations. Sometimes education is provided on site, and sometimes children are sent to local special schools. Each kind of establishment employs child care staff whose job it is to build up warm relationships with the children and cater for their general needs during out-of-school hours.

The Work of Child Care Staff

The duties of the care staff will differ according to the handicaps of the children they are dealing with. In general, they are responsible for all-round care which involves encouraging and helping with recreational activities, sharing meals with the children, caring for the children's clothes, and getting them up in the morning and putting them to bed at night. Most children live in small family groups, and the care of the living accommodation and the atmosphere created there is the responsibility of the care staff. Some domestic work can be expected, though usually cooks and cleaners are employed to do the bulk of such work.

All workers will experience some stress, though again, this will vary according to the children being cared for. With physically handicapped children, the main stress is likely to be physical. Many children may be quite helpless and must be lifted, pushed in wheelchairs, taken to the toilet and sometimes even fed. But emotionally they may be normal, happy children, so contact with them on this level can be easy and relaxed.

At the other end of the scale are schools for emotionally disturbed children. These children are often difficult to get along with, sometimes violent, and can be emotionally exhausting for those dealing with them. They will require understanding, not suppression, though it will certainly be necessary to deal with them firmly.

Mental handicaps vary so enormously that it is impossible to generalise about the stresses involved; the stresses are probably mainly physical. Many brain-damaged children remain very much like babies in their physical co-ordination as well as their mental development, and respond to being played with and cuddled in a baby-like way. But they will have the size, weight and strength of their age, and are heavy to rock, pick up and generally deal with. There are also the physically unpleasant tasks – coping with fits, incontinence and sickness, which will be part of each day's work. Where mental handicaps are also accompanied by behaviour problems, the stresses are increased and the child care staff have a demanding job.

Qualities Required

The most important thing is that you should really want to do the job and have a realistic idea of what is involved. Progress with handicapped children is often slow and therefore the rewards of the job are sometimes difficult to recognise. You must be able to accept children, whatever their handicaps, as ordinary human beings who need love and caring attention. You must respond naturally and warmly to their needs and enter fully into their life at whatever level they are able to live it. You need to be physically tough, emotionally resilient and relaxed even in difficult situations. You must be resourceful in devising leisure activities and you will find that any ability you may have with art, crafts, music, sports, etc, is useful. As you will be working as part of a team with the other child care staff, teachers and specialised professional advisers, you must be able to co-operate in a work situation and have the confidence to put across your point of view at meetings and case conferences.

Training
At basic grades no training is required, but some prior experience with children is always an advantage. It may be necessary to take further training before you are promoted to higher grades. Some organisations have their own training programmes and will also sponsor staff to take the in-service training for the Diploma in Social Work. Usually, teacher training is considered a qualification for promotion in child care work. Some larger education authorities run student schemes, employing young people on a student basis for one year during which work experience and training sessions are provided. At the end of the successful completion of this year, a permanent post is offered and the training is, of course, recognised as being a qualification for promotion. Rules and requirements for entry to student schemes vary, and enquiries should be made to the education officer of your local authority.

As children need attention around the clock, you can expect to do shift work, usually for a total of 40 hours a week. Some establishments employ separate night shift workers for the time when the children are actually in bed, so you may, or may not, have sleeping-in duties. Many schools and homes are situated in country areas and therefore provide accommodation for all staff who need it. This is less usual in cities, where there may be provision for staff only on sleeping-in duties.

Opportunities
Staff may be called residential social workers or care officers, depending on where they are employed. There are two slightly different career structures too, but in general there are four scales of responsibility, starting with assistant and working through responsibility for one family group up to responsibility for the total care staff of the establishment. Jobs are advertised, again according to the bias of the employing agency. Education authorities use their own bulletins, *The Times Educational Supplement*, and the education pages of national newspapers (eg the *Guardian* on Tuesdays). Social services departments advertise in *New Statesman and Society*, *Social Work Today*, the national press (eg 'Tomorrows' in the *Guardian* on Wednesdays), and sometimes in

local papers. Voluntary organisations may use a combination of all of these.

Case Studies

Pauline, Acting Deputy Superintendent in a Council Unit for Mentally Handicapped Children

This unit caters for eight children, and at the moment their ages range from 4 to 17. At 18 they have to leave, so we don't know what will happen to them then. We have four long-stay children and keep the other four places for short stays – that is, children who live at home but come to us during family crisis or to give their parents a bit of a rest. This kind of service can be the deciding factor for parents wondering if they can cope with a handicapped child at home. All the children are immobile and only one can talk, but most are quite able to express themselves somehow and we know when they are sad, happy, wet, angry and so on. We are not able to accept mobile children as they can be a danger to the others, not having the understanding to avoid running people down.

I have a degree and teacher training. I wanted to teach the mentally handicapped, but I did not get a job, so I came here. I am very pleased to be doing this job as I think there is more opportunity for educational work here than in a school setting. We have the children for 16 hours a day and at weekends and holidays, so we can have a great influence upon them.

All the care staff have different backgrounds. Two came here from nursing, and others had no related experience except, perhaps, in a voluntary capacity. It is amazing how all staff seem to have something to offer, whatever their background. Some with the least promising qualifications and experience have turned out to give most to the unit. They all seem to care very much about the children. One colleague who is on holiday took one of the children home with her. This child has been in care all his life and she wanted to give him the experience of being in a family. That gives you some idea of the level of commitment.

Our job description is very vague. We have to do everything for the children when the domestic staff are off duty. This means, of course, that there can be unpleasant tasks – swabbing off nappies and cleaning up sick – but frankly, you soon get used to it.

Although the kids can be difficult, it's with parents you have the most problems. You often get the brunt of their guilt and anxieties. I remember, at first, being very upset when a parent came in and complained to me about some trifling thing – something about her child's socks. But now I realise that these petty criticisms are a way of compensating for the guilt they feel at not looking after their children themselves. The worst ones are those whose children had never been away from home before they came here. Others who have previously had their kids in long-stay hospitals realise just how good this unit is, and they are appreciative.

Our strength is that, being a small unit, we can give a lot of individual attention. When the unit opened, many of the children were just blank faces. They didn't differentiate between one person and another. Now, they are responsive. One boy is starting to say one or two words and learning to use the toilet. Several have begun to feed themselves. It's great when you see progress like that.

Gillian, Assistant Care Officer

I've just started as an assistant care officer in a unit for mentally handicapped children with behaviour problems. It is a new unit and will not take the children for another two months. In the meantime, we're following a training programme, visiting homes and schools and having discussions and talks. It's a good introduction.

I don't know the reasons why people come into this work. I have done lots of things. My last job was mending sheets in a hospital. All I can say is that last night, after I had been having tea with a group of mentally handicapped children, for the first time in ages I arrived home feeling like a human being.

Sister Mary, Deputy Head (Child Care) in a Residential School for Physically Handicapped Children Run by a Voluntary Organisation

I have worked for this organisation for 22 years. When I started people came into their first job thinking of it as a life's career, but a lot of this has changed now. Girls work with us for a few years and then get married or move on. Or they have the opportunity to be transferred within our organisation and to take in-service training, so a job as a care worker is a good starting point. General conditions are changing the job, too. With higher unemployment we are getting more choice in whom we employ, and the job itself is coming to be seen differently. There is a move towards catering for handicapped children in normal schools as far as possible and offering more support to families to enable them to care for the child at home. If these ideas are widely implemented, it will change the nature of the work available with the handicapped.

Most of our care workers are young women whom we employ from the age of 18. We do occasionally get applications from men, but for various reasons we like them to be at least 21 before we employ them. Workers usually come to us unqualified, but we like them to have had experience outside school before they start. Care staff act as 'Mum', looking after a family group and doing the necessary domestic work apart from the cooking. The main strains of the job are physical – handling and lifting the children and performing intimate tasks for them. Handicapped children usually have to be washed, dressed and toileted in the same way as very young children, and care workers must be prepared for this. Many also have periods of hospitalisation and, to reduce the disruption to the child, convalescence is spent back at school. This increases the physical caring the staff must undertake. Although a lot of the work is common sense, staff must be able to carry out instructions and work as a team with the medical and education staff.

On the other hand, there is very little emotional disturbance to cope with. Most children come from stable families and visit home regularly. Any emotional difficulties tend to come from the parents, who can have strong guilt feelings at having produced a handicapped child. As the care workers, of all the staff, are closest to the children it is to them that parents often bring these difficulties. So they must be sympathetic and able to sustain this kind of contact.

The advantage of working for a voluntary organisation is that there is more stability. Staff stay longer in one job than is usually the case with local authority homes. Also, we are not subject to periodic bureaucratic reorganisations. We do, however, keep up with the times. We favour in-service training and, in this home, we run our own training programme which occupies all care staff for one morning each week. Our care staff live in, so they must be independent enough to live away from home and to fit into our community here. For those who can cope with this, it is a very friendly way of living and working.

Boarding Schools

Matron

Most boarding schools in the United Kingdom are independent and no two are alike. They may cater for boys or for girls, or be co-educational, and they range from the small, informal preparatory school, taking children between the ages of 7 and 13, to the ancient public school, founded several hundred years ago, and taking over 1,000 pupils aged between 13 and 18.

A head matron should have nursing qualifications, though only part of her job will be caring for sick children. Assistant matrons need not be qualified, but should be practical, responsible people, able to carry out instructions. It is important in these increasingly litigious times that, in the smaller schools where there is a blurring of the medical and pastoral functions, decisions as to whether a child should be referred to a doctor are taken by medically qualified staff. The larger schools tend to be divided into houses (30 to 60 children under the care of a housemaster or housemistress) and may have a sanatorium with its own nursing staff.

A matron's day starts early. Where young children are concerned she will have to get them up, probably at 7 am, and see that they wash, clean their teeth and dress neatly; she will run a morning surgery, taking temperatures and handing out pills, and cope with any sick-room cases. She is in charge of children's clothes – girls are usually expected to do their own mending – and the linen room and, although she may have to supervise cleaning staff, she will probably not be expected to do any household chores. Duties may include supervision at certain mealtimes. Matron is always on hand when children are going to bed, keeping an eye on the young ones as they bathe or shower and performing such tasks as nail cutting and hair brushing. In some schools matron sees that lights are turned out and the no-more-talking rule is obeyed. With any luck her duties will be finished at lights out, but she may be called up in the night.

Salaries vary greatly; some schools use teaching or nursing scales, others are ruled by a board of governors, who are usually not very generous. It is most important to negotiate your salary and days off and to have a clear description of your duties before you accept a job. During term the hours are long, but you can expect up to 13 weeks' holiday per year.

Qualities Required

A matron has a very special role to play in a boarding-school community; she sees a different side of the children from the teaching staff – she may, for example, be the first person to spot, and try to remedy, signs of homesickness; she can do much to create a homely atmosphere and can often act as confidante. The children's health and physical well-being are very important, so a matron needs to have, and to enforce, high standards of cleanliness and neatness. When accidents happen, she must remain calm and act promptly and competently. Jobs such as linen checking and medical record keeping call for a methodical approach. Matron must be able to get on well with housemasters, housemistresses, teaching and domestic staff, the school doctor and parents but above all, she must like, and enjoy the company of, children, who respond well to firmness tempered with kindness. The hours are long and children can be very demanding, so stamina, a mature outlook and common sense are needed, and a robust sense of humour – if you can laugh at yourself and share a joke with the children, it will get you through many a crisis.

Case Study

Dorothy, Head Matron in a Boys' Preparatory School

I'd done my basic training as a nurse and worked in a hospital for a while and I thought I wanted a change – just for a short time – so I went to work at a special school, a school for blind girls, as an assistant matron. I came here after that and have worked here for seven years now.

It is a long day. We get the boys up at 7 o'clock, which means I have to be up and dressed myself by 6.30 and awake enough to wake them up – we don't have a rising bell – and get them up and see they go to the bathroom to clean their teeth. Then I go to the surgery so that any child who needs a pill or a medicine can get it before he goes down to breakfast. The housemasters supervise breakfast while we cope with anyone who might be in the sick bay and we stay up here till after breakfast in case anyone needs surgery then. After we've had our own breakfast we do a head check for lice – lice have come back and this area is particularly bad. We do all the day children as well as the boarders; every child is looked at once a week. The boys make their own beds; there are dormitory prefects who supervise that, and when school has started we go round and see that beds and lockers are tidy and then get on with the normal laundry work and mending. We do quite a bit of washing because laundries have got so expensive and automatic washing machines are so easy, but it takes up a lot of time.

We have a cafeteria system for lunch; form teachers come in with their forms for lunch and we go down and have ours and we cope with any children in the sick bay. Sometimes this means cooking something special for them in the little kitchen we have upstairs. We do the same sort of thing in the afternoon. We have 'little tea' after school – tea and a cake or sandwich. Matrons supervise that and in the evenings it's supervising bathing, washing, showering and seeing them to bed. The youngest ones come up at quarter past seven and the last lights go out at 9.15. The housemasters turn the lights out. Then the day is finished … in theory.

Of course we have to cope with accidents that can happen at any time. You can't be a person who flaps. If someone rushes up and says 'So-and-so has cut his leg open or broken his arm', you must take it calmly. And it doesn't do to need a lot of sleep as you have a long day with an early start and you may be got up more than once in the night. But what a school matron really needs is a sense of humour.

The relationship between ourselves and the teaching staff can get a little bit fraught. Some of the games staff think we're mollycoddling the boys when they want them for a match, and this sometimes causes a little friction. I think this is a pity as we're both needed, we've both got to be here and we've both got the children's welfare at heart.

I love the response from the children. We get little ones who are a bit timid, a bit frightened coming away from home for the first time. I like seeing them grow and mature and develop their own confidence and independence. We try to make it as much like home as we can. I think a matron needs a general sort of kindliness so that she can give a child a cuddle when he needs it, without being too enveloping or pushing the parents out. I like the little ones, specially, to feel they can come up for a cuddle if they need it. The youngest ones are supposed to be almost eight, but we've had some who have just turned seven. They come with their teddy bears and pandas. No one's laughed at and it's quite accepted that if you come to sick bay your bear comes too. You really see them develop; they turn into young men, some of them, by the time they leave at 13.

Chapter 3

Working with Older Children and Young People

This chapter begins where Chapter 1 left off and covers jobs with children aged between 5 and 18 years – that is, from the time they start school to adulthood. This age range takes in the difficult period of adolescence.

Most of the jobs involve the organisation of leisure activities and, through them, the widening of the children's experience. Practical skills and an ability for sports and outdoor pastimes, therefore, play quite a large part in the work. But there are also important objectives to be achieved through the work in terms of kids' social development, their awareness of themselves and of their potential strengths and weaknesses, their ability to make sensible decisions, and so on. These are achieved through a process which can be called youth work techniques, so for most of the jobs the main training course is a two-year Youth and Community course. Playwork courses are available at Leeds Metropolitan University, Norton College and Thurrock College which provide a playwork qualification. However, this is not the only route to a job; teacher training and training for social work are normally considered suitable, and some voluntary experience is accepted in lieu of qualifications.

Youth work is often thought, by outsiders, to be unstructured. This is not really a fair criticism. The nature of the work demands a high degree of informality, but the objectives are serious and need committed and sensitive workers if they are to be achieved. To work in an unstructured way requires a high degree of skill and considerable preparatory work.

Playworkers

Playworkers provide recreational facilities for children during holidays and out-of-school hours. They usually work in a play area in a park, on an adventure playground, in a playcentre, in hospitals and other special settings, and are employed by the recreation department of a local authority, by a voluntary body or the Health

Service. The ages of the children using the play facilities are not usually laid down, but the age-range for members of the London Adventure Playground Association (LAPA) is 5-16 and the Children Act enforces clarity in this area. Working hours, of course, are much longer because of the preparation, maintenance, planning and resource management involved in the job. There are few play facilities in rural areas, so most jobs are found in the major cities.

Apart from the obvious duties of supervising behavioural and safety aspects of play, the playworker's role is to encourage personal initiative and to provide an environment which will stimulate physical, social, creative and educational play and where boredom is forgotten.

The ideal setting for playwork is the adventure playground. Often, this is a piece of land which may not look very grand but is the children's own space. It is very important, especially for city kids living in cramped conditions, because here they can safely and legitimately do such things as lighting fires, cooking camp meals, painting walls, using climbing structures, rope ladders and so on. It is central to the philosophy of adventure playgrounds that the quality of the play experience for children depends on their having control over their environment and resources.

Playworkers, who may be responsible to a management committee, or the local authority play department, are in charge of the development and maintenance of the physical provision for play on the site and must see that the site is kept clean and safe. They will have an agreed sum of money to spend on materials and equipment and will be expected to 'scrounge' from, for example, the local business community.

Playwork is about personal relationships too. Many children find it quite difficult to get along with adults and a good relationship with their playworker can help enormously. Playworkers can act as a bridge between the children and the adult world, explaining each to the other, and must, therefore, be able to relate well to both children and adults. They should encourage the involvement of interested members of the community in the operation of the playground, train voluntary workers and use their skills to the best effect. Volunteers should never be overloaded with menial or less interesting tasks or be placed in positions of sole, excessive or unfair responsibility.

Play work is demanding, both physically and emotionally. There are few comforts in the average play-hut and you will be there in all weathers. Much of the job is face-to-face contact with children, some of whom will be only too pleased to make your life difficult, and there is no career structure which will take you away from this. You may find the work very enjoyable and rewarding at first, but few people can maintain this level of personal contact indefinitely without feeling in need of a break. For all this hard work, and the variety of skills and qualities needed to do it, you will be paid a low salary with little prospect of earning more.

Opportunities

Most playworkers either work for local authorities or are funded by them. Unfortunately, many LAs are short of money and are cutting back their playwork provision. Job prospects for those who hold a Diploma (see page 107) are good; 80 per cent are in full-time work of their first choice within three months of completing the course. Some employers prefer graduates or teachers, especially those with a craft or PE background. From your own point of view, it is a good idea to start off from as broad an educational base as possible because of the lack of promotion prospects within playwork itself. When the rigours of life on the adventure playground have become too much for you, you might like to move into play recreation management, for which you may be required to hold a degree, teaching qualification or a Diploma in Social Administration.

Many playwork jobs are advertised locally, but the usual journals concerned with social welfare carry some advertisements. Seasonal, temporary work is available on many adventure playgrounds. Recruitment may be done through local recreation departments or play associations. This is a good way into permanent playwork; many playworkers started this way or by doing voluntary work.

There are opportunities for part-time work in after-school clubs and holiday play schemes, which are sometimes held on school premises but more often in parks or on housing estates. Because of the limitations imposed by the facilities available, these are less ambitious than adventure playgrounds. Sometimes teachers take these jobs, but a responsible parent or dinner lady can do the job too. Often, part-time jobs are found through personal contacts. For general information contact the National Playing Fields Association (see Useful Addresses). Information about qualifications and training for playwork is given on page 107.

Case Study

Anne, Playworker on a Council-maintained Playground

This is one of the council's show places; we've got lots of space inside and out, and we are part of a community complex which includes three associated community centres and a youth club. I think this means that we work with more of a community emphasis than many other playgrounds. The main community centre is also our administrative centre, so we keep in close contact with them and they give us a lot of support and back-up.

It's very hard to generalise about the numbers we deal with here. It is so dependent on the time of year. In the winter we can get a regular core of 25 to 30 kids aged 14-plus but fewer younger ones. But in the summer we can have anything up to 250 kids on site during the school holidays. We got depressed about the lack of kids during the winter and did a door-to-door knock-up around the estates. It seemed that weather and darkness (you have to come up dark paths to get here) were the main reasons why kids were not coming.

Although it's marvellous to have all this space, it also presents its own difficulties. There's a lot of work just maintaining the building, and outside there is so much we could do, if only we had the time and money, that sometimes it's too much to contemplate! Because of the space, the kids tend to be all over the place and it's very difficult to get quiet groups together either to talk or to carry through a particular activity. This is one of the troubles with playwork. Because of the unstructured, come-as-you-please atmosphere, it is difficult actually to achieve anything. You start a project, and next time there's a different set of kids – or perhaps they have decided they want to do something else. The middle age-group, the 13- to 15-year-olds, are the worst in this respect. But when you do actually carry something through, it's that much more worthwhile as it really has come from the kids.

I think the relationship kids can have with a playworker is very important. Most of the adults they know are people who represent some form of authority – teachers, parents, etc. But here, they can say what they like to us and come and go as they please. We only have authority through the kind of relationship we establish with them – that is if they like you, or think you are right, they will do what you say. Otherwise, it is 'Why, why, why?' all the time, and you have to come up with convincing answers!

I wanted to work with children when I left school, but didn't know about anything except teaching. I did summer work for PGL Young Adventure and then went to university. But at university I realised that was not what I wanted, so I left and was on the dole for a year. This is my first play job and I have been here 20 months now. It's very hard to see what else I can do after this. I really just want to go on doing it, but I realise that after a while you need a break, although I haven't reached that point yet!

Youth and Community Work

Whereas playwork is primarily a recreation job, youth and community work is geared towards social education and is financed mainly by local education authorities. Most authorities employ a youth and community officer who is responsible for co-ordinating the work in the area, and there will be a team of youth workers to carry out the tasks. As well as this statutory provision there is a strong voluntary movement, eg the YMCA, YWCA, Youth Clubs UK, National Association of Boys' Clubs, often partly financed by the local education authorities but operating independently. The scope and settings of youth and community work have widened a great deal in recent years. You might, for example, work in an agency encouraging young people to undertake community service, in a counselling service, on a project for the young unemployed, on a juvenile justice work programme or, as a community educator, be based in a village or community college. Wherever you are, you will find yourself dealing principally with young people aged between 14 and 17.

Centre-based and Detached Workers

There are two main kinds of job: club- or centre-based, and detached. If you are in charge of a club or centre, you will probably be the only professional in the unit, though you could have under you a team of part-time workers, specialist instructors and caretaking staff. Part of your time will be spent in face-to-face work with individuals or groups of young people and part of it arranging club events. A management committee normally provides support in the administration work. A detached worker does not have a physical base but goes out into the community to talk to the kids in the streets, the cafes, the discos and wherever else they congregate. He or she must make contact with kids who for one reason or another do not want to come to a club, and must know the area well because this is the working arena.

Both these kinds of workers have the same basic aim – to help the adolescents they deal with to develop social skills and good personal relationships and grow up with a greater awareness of themselves and their society. There is a trend towards greater professionalism now that the importance of counselling is recognised.

As a youth worker you must, first of all, be able to establish yourself as an adult friend with whom all kinds of things can be discussed freely. You must, of course, have a good knowledge of the way society and our political system work, and you must also know the local community well. You do not 'teach' in any formal sense but you should be able to impart information and stimulate discussion in an informal way so that the kids you work with can make judgements for themselves. Leisure management is also an important aspect of the work, as it is the failure to use leisure time constructively that often leads kids into trouble. Your role may be to provide the right kind of activities at your own centre, or to direct kids to suitable activities available elsewhere in the community. Either way, you need to know your kids well and have good local contacts in places where their needs might be met.

A first job can carry considerable responsibilities; a newly qualified applicant should, therefore, try to find out exactly what these responsibilities are and whether or not there will be adequate support available, at least to begin with. There is a probationary year to serve before you can be registered as a fully qualified practitioner. Some local authorities and the larger voluntary organisations have a Youth and Community Service training officer who will provide induction and in-service training as part of a staff development scheme.

Qualifications and Training
Details are set out on pages 102–106. Some courses require prior experience and this can be gained through part-time paid or voluntary work. Your local youth officer at the education department should be able to help you find a paid job, and if you want to do voluntary work the local Volunteer Bureau (if there is one) can give you information. Otherwise, a general enquiry to a voluntary organisation such as Youth Clubs UK should be helpful.

A few local authorities employ unqualified workers in full-time posts, and although the pay is poor and career prospects limited, this would be a good way of getting pre-training experience on a salary.

Conditions of Work, Pay and Prospects
Because of the informal nature of the work, much of it is done during evenings and at weekends and it is easy to work beyond your set hours. There are also considerable pressures involved in the face-to-face contact with kids. The career structure is still fairly limited, though better than it used to be. There is now greater mobility between the voluntary and statutory sectors, career prospects exist at regional or national level and salary scales compare favourably with those of related jobs. However, most people find there is a limit to the number of years they can cope with the tensions produced by working full-time with young people in informal situations.

There are set salary scales agreed by a joint negotiating committee, the JNC, for all holders of recognised qualifications. These are slightly lower than teaching scales.

Jobs are advertised in the social work and education journals as well as in the local press, *Time Out* and the *Guardian* (Wednesdays). The National Youth Agency has publications which are a valuable source of information and contain job advertisements.

Youth and Community Officers
Youth and community officers are employed by local education authorities or voluntary agencies to advise their committees on the staffing, planning and maintenance of the service, to see that their decisions are implemented and to co-ordinate the work of full- and part-time voluntary and professional staff. There is no formal qualifying training for youth and community officers. The work calls for administrative and counselling skills, and wide experience of young people both inside and outside the education service.

Case Study

Sheila, Youth Worker at a Voluntary Youth Club

I have a degree, but no youth qualifications. I started out as a playleader but decided that I wanted to work with older kids in a more structured situation. I did voluntary youth work at first, then I got some paid sessional work, and finally was taken on by this club as a full-time worker. That was when the local education authority took over responsibility for salary payments.

Although the boundaries between playleadership and youth work are loosely defined, I prefer working for the education service as I do now. It indicates your starting point. You see yourself as part of a wider education system and your training and professional groups have a different emphasis. Youth work is very much concerned with social and political education – there's a general shift nowadays away from the skittles and the table tennis towards project-based work. There's a recognition of the need to work with ethnic minorities and to tackle issues such as unemployment.

This is a black club and most of our workers are black. The kids have divided themselves. Both black and white want their own space and they don't want to share it. A couple of years ago we saw the way things seemed to be going, and decided we ought to employ more black workers. Soon the division was complete. Although I support the kids' decision to divide themselves in this way, I think that there is room for a white worker like me in a black club. I am a white adult they can relate to, who is not in authority. And the other workers, especially the part-timers, come mainly from the kids' own community or are former club members or local parents – so we don't have a problem with seeing workers as professionals from outside.

As we are a voluntary group, with a local management committee, we have almost complete autonomy and can take the club in whatever direction we wish. Our emphasis has been on girls, as most youth clubs are dominated by boys. We have a girls-only after-school club and a weekly girls' night, when the girls have an opportunity to learn skills without being inhibited by the boys' presence. We find that they are then able to play a stronger role in the general sessions.

We've also had a lot of our girls getting pregnant, so we have started working with a young mothers' group so that we can build up a system of support within which they can help each other with child care.

Juvenile Justice Work

Juvenile justice work, previously known as intermediate treatment, is an attempt to reduce delinquency in children and young people aged between 7 and 17. Most local authorities have juvenile justice services but they may be provided in partnership with voluntary agencies and the Education or Probation services. The kinds of children referred to schemes are those who are suffering from the effects of poor family relationships and are perhaps lacking in positive adult attention and are consequently unmotivated and unable to relieve their own boredom and frustration. Many regularly play truant, start to underachieve, become disruptive and then begin to offend, resulting in convictions.

There are two kinds of work in juvenile justice, full time and sessional. Full-time workers administer and develop schemes and nowadays spend an increasing amount of time dealing with juvenile justice issues and working with the police and the courts. Sessional work might be one-to-one counselling or organising a range of group activities such as camping, kite flying or doing up an old car. Most schemes run evening sessions and children attend two or three times a week, but some operate day-time centres where children with school problems can receive some form of alternative education.

If you do juvenile justice work it must be geared towards the total aims of the schemes you are working on. You will most probably be functioning as a social worker, but you will have very specific aims, knowing that if you fail to achieve some stability or improvement in the children you work with, they may be taken into care or go to court. You will have to monitor the effectiveness of the scheme and the individual progress of the children with whom you are involved. In most schemes there is a place for people from a wide range of backgrounds: teaching, social work, leisure and recreation, community work, craft work; and volunteers willing to do befriending have an important contribution to make. The qualifications required vary from employer to employer; many accept relevant work experience in lieu of formal qualifications. But if you are looking for training, a DipSW course is the best all-round choice. Pay is usually in line with the pay scales used by the employer.

You must expect evening work, as most sessions take place in the evening, and you must be prepared to attend residential weekends and accompany children on holidays. Few schemes are fortunate enough to have purpose-built accommodation so work is often carried out with improvised equipment and on premises that are far from ideal.

Jobs are advertised in *Social Work Today*, *Community Care* and the *Guardian* (Wednesdays).

The National Association for the Care and Resettlement of Offenders (NACRO)

NACRO, a registered charity and company limited by guarantee, employs about 1,000 staff in over 100 workplaces in England and Wales. Staff are organised in specialised teams, each of which provides a range of services. All NACRO's work is devoted to developing more humane and effective ways of dealing with crime. Its projects are in the fields of housing, employment training, youth training, advice, education, resettlement and crime prevention. It also provides research, information and training services for people concerned about crime and offenders. It works in close co-operation with other national and local agencies and with local communities.

NACRO does not have a 'career structure'. Its staff do not need to have social work qualifications, but bring in a range of relevant skills and experience. Salaried posts are advertised regularly in the *Guardian* (Wednesdays).

NACRO New Careers Training

NACRO's New Careers Training develops and runs youth training schemes for young offenders and young people at risk of getting into trouble, whose needs may not be met by the general YT. There are currently about 20 such schemes offering approximately 2,000 places. A trainee joins for two years and is paid a training allowance. Many of the trainees are disadvantaged school-leavers, of whom a high proportion have already appeared before the courts. They receive counselling and personal support, enabling them to take full advantage of a demanding work-based training, and are offered learning opportunities in such areas as literacy and numeracy, confidence building and problem solving.

Case Study

Lynn, a Co-ordinator in one of NACRO's New Careers Training Centres

I left school with A levels, went to a college of further education and got a teacher's certificate and did voluntary work with young people with learning difficulties. My first job was doing youth training for the educationally disadvantaged – children from special schools or slow learners; I taught them needlecraft.

I then joined NACRO. My induction course included management skills and techniques, counselling skills and administration and working with difficult youngsters. It was very useful. My transition to co-ordinator was quite rapid. Although a co-ordinator has overall responsibility for a scheme and its aims, I still work with the trainees.

NACRO has an open-door policy and all sorts of trainees get referred to us. Some may be offenders, or risk becoming offenders. They may not want to join the scheme, but sometimes they're referred by the court or probation. It's very rewarding when you can do a court report and stop kids going inside because they're on your scheme and you can prove they're working and attending every day. A lot of our trainees are socially disadvantaged. They have all sorts of problems at home – parents may be out of work, one or both parents may have drink problems, there may be drug abuse – and some of them have been in care. When we get trainees who can't read or write, we put on literacy and numeracy classes for them. We had one girl who took her GCSEs at the end of the year, which was a great achievement for someone who had not managed to get the lowest grade CSE at school.

I think they're all lacking in confidence – they've failed at school, they may have failed on other schemes, and we offer a last hope. We try to provide a scheme that will meet their needs. When they join, we ask them why they've come and they nearly all say it's to learn a skill. They want the work experience, they want to be able to get a job at the end of it. They know they can't go on as they are. We give them the workshop training and get them the placements, and many of them get City and Guilds certificates as well as their YT certificate. But they need a lot of other help too. We give health and safety training, we do team-building exercises, we try to help them improve their personal effectiveness. They video themselves when we simulate job interviews and we all have a good laugh.

Anyone doing this job needs a lot of understanding: understanding of the needs of young people, of what their problems are, of what's going on in the community, of the latest developments in criminal justice, of the problems of ethnic minorities, of the gay community – of all sorts of things. You need patience and determination too, because you have to keep motivating them, keep encouraging them. You can't insist on things like timekeeping when they first come, it's enough to get them just to attend. You do a lot of listening and counselling. You're dealing with difficult kids, they're street-wise and quite prepared to be argumentative, so a sense of humour is pretty essential. You must be able to communicate, not only with the trainees – you have to be able to talk their language – but with people outside NACRO and, of course, with your colleagues, as this is very much team work.

Youth Training (YT)

YT, a government programme funded through local Training and Enterprise Councils (TECs), offers 16- and 17-year-old school-leavers a placement which provides work experience and both on-the-job and off-the-job training. Placements are in industrial or commercial firms, on farms, on community projects or with any other employer who can offer supervised work experience. The scheme is open to young people in a job, to apprentices and to those who are out of work. The scheme may be called by a different name in some areas, for example Network.

Trainees

Trainees are paid a weekly allowance and, on successful completion of the programme, receive an NVQ. If you join the scheme and then feel you have opted for the wrong programme, you are free to leave at any time, or you can sometimes switch to another programme.

If you apply to work with children, you will probably be given a placement on one of the caring skills programmes and could work, for example, in a nursery.

Projects and Posts

In areas of high unemployment, where businesses are being closed down and adult employees are being made redundant, there are unfortunately not enough employer-based placements to meet demand and a number of special schemes have been set up.

YT Placement Supervisors

A YT placement supervisor finds potential work placements, and then, in conjunction with the employer offering the placement, sets up a training programme. While the trainees are on the placement, the supervisor offers them guidance and support, monitors their progress and makes sure that the programme is being followed through. To be a placement officer you need a very thorough knowledge of the area in which your local YT operates, and good communication skills, as you will have to explain to both trainer and trainee what is expected of them. For information about training, see page 105.

Employment Training

Anyone aged between 18 and 59 who has been unemployed for more than six months is eligible to enter the programme. Priority is given to those aged between 18 and 24 who have been unemployed for between six and twelve months and those aged between 18 and 50 who have remained unemployed for over two years, and the groups for whom special arrangements are made include disabled people and women returning to the labour market.

If you are interested in working with children or young people, your practical training might take you into a playgroup or nursery. The scheme offers up to one year's training to help prepare you for work. Your interests and skills are assessed by an independent local training agent, an action plan is drawn up for you and then a training manager organises your training, which takes place both on and off the job. After training you will receive a record of your achievement on the programme and many trainees obtain a recognised vocational qualification or credit towards one. For details contact your local Jobcentre or Training Enterprise Council.

Careers Officers

Most careers officers are employed by local education authorities (LEA), but a number (usually those with experience of commerce or industry) work in university and college careers and appointments services. Experience of commerce and industry is useful in both situations. Additionally, many careers officers have previous experience in teaching.

LEA careers officers are based in offices open to members of the public and their clients are in the age range 14 to 20. Much of their time is spent interviewing young people, sometimes accompanied by a parent, and giving them information and guidance on careers, education and training. Their work is supported by employment assistants who take vacancy details and arrange interviews and undertake the day-to-day operation of careers offices with the help of clerical staff.

Careers officers also visit schools and colleges of further education where they organise discussion groups, talk to students about the national and local career options open to them and provide individual occupational guidance. They work closely with careers teachers and other staff in schools, advising on the careers programmes, the availability of careers information and contacts with employers, including work experience, and assisting with careers-related aspects of the curriculum.

Careers officers are aware of the problems and pressures that young people have to face, and are able to listen sympathetically as well as explain things clearly and simply. Many people who go to a careers office need more than just careers counselling; they may, for example, be homeless or dependent on drugs; careers officers have to know which agencies will be able to help their clients and, in some cases, persuade the clients to seek help. Careers officers must build up good working relationships with many agencies as well as school careers teachers and employers.

There is a certain amount of administrative work attached to the job, eg the keeping of records and interview notes, and many services hold this information on computerised systems. Careers officers use questionnaires to help to identify pupils' abilities and aspirations. Other tasks include preparing talks, producing information leaflets, arranging visits and supervising the work of support staff. Some careers officers specialise in helping certain groups of clients, eg those with learning problems, ethnic minorities, college students. Each LEA careers service is organised on a geographical basis and there are opportunities to gain managerial responsibility by working as a team leader, or district or area officer. Trained LEA careers officers can move into university careers advisory work, social services training or personnel work. The professional qualification for the careers service is the Diploma in Careers Guidance (DCG) – see page 105. The employment assistant does not need professional qualifications but should possess good interviewing skills.

Commercial Children's Holidays

If you enjoy outdoor life, an attractive, but rarely permanent, job can be found with commercial firms offering holidays to unaccompanied children and school groups. The requirements and conditions of employment will vary slightly from firm to firm, but the larger and more reputable ones work to a high standard and will provide an equally good working situation. Most cater for children aged from 7 to 18 years and all operate from Easter until September. Staff are required for every aspect of the holidays, from administration and catering to maintenance of equipment, but the main jobs involving contact with the children are those of group organiser, courier and instructor.

The Work of the Group Organiser

Group organisers work with small groups of children who are holidaying alone or with friends. They are responsible for the general welfare of the children at all times when they are not involved in a specific supervised activity. They have an important role to play in making sure that everyone enjoys the holiday and that spare time is spent constructively. They must help all the children in their group get along together, deal with any personal problems and make sure that the quieter ones are not left out.

Group organisers need a strong, likeable personality, the ability to generate a party spirit among the children, and lots of ideas for making the holiday fun.

The Work of the Courier

Most holiday firms offer supervised travel from major cities to the holiday centre. Couriers are employed for this, and must therefore be capable of this kind of supervision, as accidents can easily happen if things get out of hand. Couriers are also employed to assist school groups which will have their own teachers for dealing with general supervision and personal attention, but may need help with arrangements for outings and general use of the amenities offered at the holiday centre.

The Work of the Instructor

Children's holidays are based on a range of outdoor activities in which instruction and supervision are given. Activities will vary according to the amenities of the holiday location, but commonly include hill walking, pony trekking, archery, canoeing, sailing, snorkelling and farm holidays. Some firms give special sports coaching holidays too.

If you have considerable experience of an activity of this kind and if, in addition, you have some instructional or teaching experience, you can apply for a job as an instructor. You must be capable of coping with complete beginners, as most of the children will have no experience, and you must be aware of the safety requirements for your activity. For instance, if you wish to be an instructor in any watersports, you must be a good swimmer and have proven life-saving ability.

The approach to the work is to make the activity fun, rather than to aim for high standards, and you must be prepared to work in this way. Your ability to establish easy personal relationships with children will be important.

Conditions of Work

There are holiday centres throughout the British Isles, often in beautiful parts of the country or near the sea. Some British firms run holidays abroad, particularly in France. American firms employ people for the summer months on contracts which include payment of return air fare and a fortnight's free time in America.

Most jobs with holiday firms are seasonal, and the average length of employment is six weeks. But it is possible to work, at a peak period, for one week only, or to be employed for the whole season. You will usually be employed on a contract which states clearly the conditions of employment and the reasons for which you can be dismissed. As you will be working closely with children for whom the firm has responsibility, there are usually strict rules about such things as alcohol consumption, smoking and drugs, and to break these can mean instant dismissal.

You will be given accommodation of the type available to the children, which may be in cabins, tents or purpose-built huts, but you cannot expect a tent or room to yourself. Your meals will be provided and usually you will eat with the children – comradeship is the keynote of these holidays. You will be paid a weekly allowance or pocket money, and sometimes there may be bonus payments for any relevant qualifications you possess. Some firms will pay your travelling expenses to and from the holiday centre, particularly if this is abroad. You will have a specified amount of free time.

Qualifications

Firms rely heavily on teachers and social workers or students expecting to enter this kind of work. But anyone who has experience with children, in youth clubs, play schemes or other areas, can apply. If you wish to work as an instructor, you must have good experience in your chosen activity.

Most firms start sending out information and application forms in January when the mass of holiday advertising begins in the national press. They may not actually appoint staff until March or later. Appointments are often made on the strength of the application form and references, as interviewing would involve applicants in considerable travel. Most firms, however, are ready to talk to interested people on the phone and answer any questions they may have.

Firms seldom advertise for staff, but as all of them need to make new appointments each year it is reasonable to write to those whose holidays you see advertised in the national press or by travel agents to ask what opportunities for employment they have. As holiday jobs are popular with teachers and students, you may stand a better chance of employment if you are free to work outside the school, college and university holidays.

Other Leisure Work

Leisure centres, and amusement and theme parks, which are now found in increasing numbers throughout the UK, all attract crowds of children and young people and offer a wide range of (mostly seasonal) employment. Those who run such places require management skills and business acumen and very often hold a business or recreational management qualification, but ride operators, costume staff and attendants do not need professional qualifications and are hired because they possess stamina, pleasant extrovert personalities and the capacity to help people enjoy themselves. You could find yourself supervising children in a paddling pool, driving a miniature railway engine or dressed up in a Mickey Mouse suit, being photographed with young fans. Should you decide that you like the holiday atmosphere but that too much close client contact palls after a while, you could take one of several training courses related to the leisure industry and move into administration. Certificates and diplomas are awarded by City and Guilds and the Institute of Leisure and Amenity Management.

Chapter 4

Special Projects

During the past 15 years or so, there has been a strong movement towards ordinary people taking part in the provision and organisation of their local amenities. This community spirit has launched many projects which offer support and resources to community groups or which aim to compensate for particular areas of deprivation.

Most projects are set up and run by voluntary groups and staffed by paid community workers, usually with the help of a local authority grant, and many are now fighting to maintain their existence at a time of expenditure cuts.

The ideal running through these projects is that of self-help and community involvement – the belief that people should do their own thing. Special projects can cover a wide field. The ones described here are a fairly representative handful which give some idea of the range of activity and opportunity in this area.

Parent and Toddler Workers

Although the network of a good social services department can spread far and wide, no provision is made for parents with children under three unless they are taken, as a priority case, to a local day centre. For many families, the time when the children are youngest is also the time of greatest stress. Parents are new to childrearing, nights may be broken and they may feel isolated at home with a small child. Statistics have shown that a large percentage of women at home with young children suffer from some form of depression which, of course, affects the family as a whole.

It has been left to voluntary groups to tackle these problems by setting up parent and toddler groups where parents and their young children can go to meet others in the same situation. These groups are usually run by the parents who use them, who often have little experience of what they are doing and are uncertain of what exactly they want to achieve. So, in some areas, grants have made possible the employment of a parent and toddler worker who can act as an adviser to the groups, help them sort out their problems and, if they are interested, broaden their horizons. The work may be done in close association with the local PPA or social services, but essentially the worker is the servant of the voluntary sector – of the individual parent and toddler groups in the area.

Case Study

Wendy, Parent and Toddler Worker

I am employed for $17\frac{1}{2}$ hours a week, and my work covers the whole of the borough. The job divides into three areas – educational work, literature and contact with the parent and toddler groups.

I had no training in any formal sense. After I left school I travelled and did odd jobs, and I came into this job via community work which I began on a voluntary basis. I gave up community work when my baby was born, and when he was a year old I applied for this job, thinking the part-time work would be ideal. In practice, it didn't work out that way. I am involved with between 30 and 40 different groups and the task can be endless. At first, it was very difficult when I had to take the baby with me. He wasn't old enough to be socially independent. Now he is two, things are easier as he likes being with other children and will settle down with them when I visit groups.

My work is not clearly defined. It involves scouting around a bit, visiting the parent and toddler groups which are independent and self-running, and seeing how they are getting on. If I see any general weaknesses I try to set up something to counter them. At the moment I'm organising a course on the first two years of life, aimed at expectant mums and parents of very young children. I am also beginning a play project which can be taken to groups. We already have a toy library and a set of soft play equipment which can be booked by groups who want to use it. It is up to the individual groups to decide whether they want to use these facilities. It is not my job to spoonfeed them, or force them in directions they do not want to take.

I am also involved in producing literature which I think might be helpful. Most recently, I've put together a guide to setting up and running a parent and toddler group. And there's always the business of publicity – posters and handbills – so that people know what's going on and what's available. I do most of this myself, though sometimes I do get help.

At first, I felt very isolated in this job and felt the lack of colleagues with whom I could discuss aims and achievements. I still feel isolated in the sense that I don't share the responsibility with anyone, but I'm now more confident of the direction I want the work to take and I am known by the parent and toddler groups and the other under-twos workers in the area. Although I work alone, I come into contact with a great variety of people.

Community Resource Centres

Centres are located in inner city areas and aim, broadly speaking, to help local community groups to achieve their objectives. They do this through offering three main types of service. First, they have resources which can be used free of charge. These could include a double-decker bus which can go where it is needed and be used for anything from a play session to a councillor's 'surgery', printing facilities, equipment for social activities, crafts kits and video and sound recording equipment. Second, they run an information service of a kind likely to be useful to community groups; and finally, they organise workshops where groups can learn skills which will help them to run their own activities.

A centre is run democratically by a team of workers who each have their own specialist area, but also take their share of all the necessary tasks. They regard themselves as community workers and are dedicated to the ideal of self-help. A lot of their time is spent working with children and young people in parent and toddler groups, holiday play schemes, youth clubs and so on.

Case Study

Pam, Under-fives Worker

Although I am the under-fives worker here, I probably don't spend more than a day and a half in any one week working strictly in my specialist area. It is my responsibility to initiate and co-ordinate the work we do with young children, but once a project is set up we all help out with running it. We work as a collective, all sharing the work and taking equal turns with administration, cleaning, supervision and education in the use of the printing equipment, lending out resources and so on.

We are interested in development work. For instance, using our play bus, we recently established a Two O'Clock Club, and now that is going well we just keep in contact with one weekly visit. We liaise with many community groups and offer various kinds of support. We help to initiate projects on adventure playgrounds and each worker has one session of contact youth work a week. We take crafts and video equipment to groups, not as a one-off activity but in the hope that the playleaders will afterwards be able to organise similar projects for themselves. Although most of our work is connected with children, we often have more contact with the workers than with the kids. A lot of time is spent liaising with the workers and attending meetings.

I got my job because of the extent of my experience, rather than for any qualifications I have. I have been involved with a lot of voluntary work. I have worked with the disabled, with alcoholics and on adventure play schemes. I also did therapy work in a hospital. Some of this work was unpaid, and for some I received a salary. It is amazing the experience you can come by in this way.

City Farms and Community Gardens

City Farms and Community Gardens are community projects which offer facilities and opportunities for training, education, work and recreation to the very young, the elderly, the disabled and mentally handicapped, youths and adults of all abilities and backgrounds.

Four city farms started up in London in 1972 and there are now over 60 widely scattered over the British Isles. City farms concentrate on farm animals and gardening; city gardens are similar but on smaller sites and have no livestock. They are sited on what was once derelict land and reintroduce some sort of ecological balance to urban areas. All are the result of independent local group effort and the emphasis is on active involvement rather than watching other people do things. Older children have the opportunity for regular day-to-day contact and involvement in farm-type activities. For the less academically inclined child these regular visits (both in and out of school) and the contact with animals and people in a relaxed, supportive but work-like environment are an important stimulus to their personal development.

Most city farms can draw on expertise from such locally-based professionals as vets, solicitors and teachers and will employ three or four specialist workers to manage the farm and its various activities. Some staff are animal or horticultural experts, others have training in youth and community work as working with children is a major part of the job. Some city farms have large parties of visiting schoolchildren several times a week; coping with their demands can be stressful, but is nearly always intensely rewarding. A number of city farms sponsor youth training and employment projects.

Job applications must be made to individual farms. The address of the National Federation of City Farms is on page 111.

Case Study

Bob, Youth Worker on a City Farm

We have four workers here and although we all come from different backgrounds, and therefore have different skills, we all take the same salary. No one is really in charge. One of the workers was a farmer, one is experienced with horses and one is an instructor who does special work with disabled kids. I am the youth worker. I had never worked with animals before I came here. I ran a youth team and before that did some public relations work for a while.

We try to cater for as wide a range of people as possible. We do a lot of work with disabled kids and have special facilities for horse-riding for physically handicapped children. Our emphasis is upon education. The farm is effectively run by 20 or 30 local kids who do the work with our support. We teach them all they need to know, and really I think they could manage the place alone if necessary, that is, as far as the physical care of the animals is concerned.

Every farm has its particular emphasis. Ours is horses and we are quite structured in this direction. We take in some liveries which, incidentally, helps with the finances, and the kids take the British Horse

Society Instruction Course which qualifies them to teach riding or to run a riding stable. It gives them the opportunity to do something different from serving behind a shop counter. And with the development of the city farm movement, there are career prospects here too.

To work here you need to have a liking for the concept of the project. There are lots of schemes now which are basically about putting life into a community. This is one way of doing it - and a very effective way.

Children's Theatre

In the past, children might have expected to see a pantomime at Christmas and a Punch and Judy show while on a seaside holiday. Today, they have a far richer and more varied choice of entertainment. Many of the major repertory companies have a young people's theatre attached to them, and groups and individual entertainers often play to children in schools, libraries and parks and even on the streets during neighbourhood festivals. The movement to take drama out of theatres in order to reach a wider audience is based on the belief that entertainment has an educational and social role to play.

If you are interested in children's theatre, you will find that three main opportunities exist: with theatre groups, puppet groups, and solo performance. Whichever way you work, you will probably want to encourage an active response from the children and involve them in the entertainment. Some performers take the idea of audience involvement a stage further, stepping into what is called participatory drama, where the children are no longer the audience but take part in the drama even to the extent of deciding how the plot will develop. This kind of theatre requires you to be more than a performer. You must be able to interact with the children in a sensitive and constructive way.

Qualities Required

Many children's theatre groups operate on a shoestring and all members of the company contribute to all aspects of the work. If you are a solo performer you will write your own script and make your own costumes, props and puppets, and you may do much the same if you work with a group. So you must be versatile and able to turn your hand to a variety of tasks. As a performer, you must be able to establish rapport with the children and be aware of techniques for gaining a response and, when necessary, controlling it. The ability to improvise is important too, so that you can draw the children's contribution into the show without losing control of the plot. If you are involved with any script-writing, you need a fairly intimate knowledge of the kinds of subject children will respond to at different ages - when they like pure fantasy, when they are amused by everyday objects in bizarre situations, when they will thrill to the eternal battle of the goodies and baddies, and when they will take an interest in real life issues. This, like most of the qualities which go to make up a good children's entertainer, comes with constant contact with the children. You must respond to them just as much as they do to you.

Training and Job Finding

There is no direct training for children's theatre. Some people take teacher training courses and specialise in drama, some go to drama school, and others come into the work after experience in amateur groups. Some young people's theatre groups give opportunities for voluntary work, and larger community arts organisations some- times run short drama and puppetry courses. A report on the feasibility of a full-time training course in professional puppet theatre is available from The Puppet Centre at £5. Interchange Trust in London run a community drama course each summer which offers experience of working with children in a variety of ways.

If you feel ready to begin work you have the choice of setting up as a solo performer or joining a group. To work on your own needs a good deal of confidence and resourcefulness and some money. You will need to advertise yourself to potential customers such as local schools, recreation departments and community centres. But remember that it is necessary to get the permission of the relevant authority before you do so. If you would like to join a group, you may wait a long time if you rely on advertisements. Some groups advertise in journals like the *Stage* and *Time Out*, but most recruit through personal contact, so direct enquiries are probably the best. The Puppet Centre or Interchange Trust may be able to help with general enquiries.

Case Studies

Alex Howard, Puppeteer
I first started as a solo performer. I had no money and no car and had to carry all my stuff on the Underground. But this was the best training I could have had because I had to learn everything.

I saved some money and spent it on publicity which I sent to schools and recreation departments. So I began performing in schools, parks and libraries, and also at private birthday parties. Once you start performing, the thing snowballs as one person recommends you to another. One birthday party I did was at the house of a TV director. That was a piece of luck because that was how we landed our first television contract.

Later, I joined up with a friend and we formed this company, which has grown over 10 years to the nine members we now have. We take our shows all over the place, performing in theatres and schools, and we also do some work for television. I enjoy working in schools best because there we have really close contact with the children and it is easy to establish rapport with them. It can be tremendously rewarding because children seem to find puppets easy to identify with and they can respond to them with a freedom which can be repressed in other circumstances. They often interrupt to tell the puppets something about themselves, and we always respond to their comments.

My first sustained experience of working with children was when I took a holiday workshop in puppetry. I realised very quickly that I had to establish myself as a friend, but also to be in charge. I learnt a lot about children during the fortnight and I certainly learnt to appreciate their humour. All the children made a puppet of a character of their own choice and at the end we wove them into a show. One child with a bad stammer had made a monster and, against the advice of the others, I decided he should perform in the show. As it turned out, he did it without any stammer – he was hiding behind his puppet character.

I do the writing for our company. When we first began I did adaptations of traditional stories, and then a friend suggested that I should use my own ideas. I have a child-like mind anyway, so I began to draw upon my own imagination and the stories just emerged. I try to keep the language very simple as I write mainly for very young children. Most of the stories draw upon everyday objects and situations, but I make them magical or fantastic. I think young children want fantasy, not social realism.

Some people think that we arrived when we got our first television contract. It was certainly flattering, and an opportunity to really concentrate on the artistic aspect of the shows – there has been a lot of bad puppetry about and it felt good to be doing it well. But, looking back, I realise the early successes were the most exciting.

Richard, Member of a Community Theatre Group

This company is part of a wider Community Arts organisation and we specialise in participatory theatre. This means that our dramas are only very loosely constructed by us and we involve the kids in them. The plot is our fall-back position and we can spread out from there according to the children's response and abilities. We work mainly with theatre in the round so that there is no barrier between us and the kids. We also do quite a lot of follow-up work when we split off into groups with the kids and discuss or elaborate on the show on the level of the particular group. We do teachers' packs as well which can be used in a similar way.

We work with a wide age range. In the schools we deal mainly with the under-11s, but on adventure playgrounds and holiday playschemes the ages can go much higher. We find that above the age of about 13 it is difficult to work in our usual way, so we involve the older ones on a video project, filming what the younger ones are doing.

The main drawback is that the work is heavy. I work a demanding schedule and I'm not just a performer. I'm interacting with the kids. You get a lot of feedback from them and they generate a lot of energy. Children are not guarded or non-committal in their response. In parks and on playgrounds they will leave if they don't like what you are doing. We find that we need to use different tactics for dealing with each situation. For instance, on adventure playgrounds we perform on high ground away from the play equipment to gain our audience. In schools and nurseries, where children can be controlled, we have to work harder to get a response but we do get it. Response is essential to the progression of the entertainment.

Working in this way is heavy on technique. There are ways of talking to the children to get them going. We begin with closed questions which only need a yes or no answer and then move on to the why? and how? questions. We have to be in control without resorting to repression. Disrupters usually have a reason for making a noise, so we try to take notice of them and act on their suggestions. We rarely say 'no'. At the end of the performance, we unmask. This is part of the process of bringing the kids down again and it is very important. You can only responsibly involve kids in uninhibited action if you can bring about a return to 'normality' at the end.

Chapter 5

Voluntary Work

Many people who take up the kinds of job described in this book have their first contact with children through voluntary work. This is often the best way, both of gaining experience which may be needed for admission to a training course or for employment, and of finding out what working with children is really like. Not everybody is able to respond easily to children and find the right balance between easy communication and discipline. However much you feel that you want to work with children, it is a good idea to get some first-hand experience before embarking on training or your first paid job.

There are two main ways of gaining experience through voluntary work and your choice will depend largely on your age and situation. First, you can work locally and part time while still at school or holding down a job. No money is involved in work of this kind as you do it in your spare time and it should not affect any other commitments you have. Second, you can work as a full-time volunteer in return for accommodation and pocket money.

Spare-time Work

As this kind of work must be fitted in with the rest of your life it should be conveniently near your home, so your choice will depend on what is available locally. It will also depend on your own particular attitudes and interests. For instance, if you are a churchgoer you may find work through your local church, and if you feel sympathetic towards the Scout and Guide movement, contact your local scout and guide companies. If you want general information before making a decision, contact your local Volunteer Bureau, if there is one, or the Citizens' Advice Bureau or social services department if there isn't. It is a good idea to arrange your voluntary work through a Volunteer Bureau, as you will get help in making your choice and may also get some support from the workers at the bureau while you are on the job.

Just because you are volunteering your services it does not mean that you will be free to work only on your own terms. Workers, whether they are paid or not, must be reliable if the activities of the organisation are to proceed successfully. It is just as important for voluntary workers to turn up regularly, work in co-operation with others and carry out instructions, as it is for paid staff. So, when you are deciding on voluntary work, you must ask for a clear account of what will be expected of you, and make sure that you can commit yourself to it. If you are still at school or have family responsibilities, you must see to it that your attendance is not broken every time you have an essay to write or you get behind with household tasks. Once in a while, on the night before an important exam, or if your child should become ill, you can expect to miss your duties. But you should always make sure that people know in advance, so that other arrangements can be made.

At what age can you begin voluntary work? This depends on the ages of the children you will be helping, as it is usually necessary for you to be older than they are. The younger the children, the sooner you can start. You may remember that one of the girls whose case studies appear in Chapter 1 began Sunday School teaching with very young children when she was 13. This is probably the youngest age at which voluntary work can usefully begin.

There is one slightly different type of spare-time voluntary work which is worth a separate mention. This is holiday work. Many children's and youth groups, especially those in large cities, arrange country camping holidays for their kids and need extra help. The holidays usually last for a week or a fortnight and helpers can expect to be paid their expenses. Provided you have the time to spare, this is a good way of acquiring concentrated experience of what it is like to be with kids around the clock. It can also be an enjoyable, if busy, holiday for you.

Examples of Organisations Needing Part-time Helpers

With under-fives
Parent and Toddler Groups
Nurseries and Playgroups
Sunday School Teaching
Nursery Groups for
    Disabled Children

With older children
Cubs and Brownies
Woodcraft
Sunday School Teaching
Play schemes and Adventure
    Playgrounds

Holiday Camping
Clubs for Disabled Children

With teenagers
Scouts and Guides
Boys' and Girls' Brigades
Youth Clubs
Adventure Playgrounds
Holiday Camping
Clubs for Disabled
    Teenagers
Juvenile Justice
    Projects

Full-time Work: CSV

If you have just left school, finished a course of higher education, or are considering a change of career, you may decide to do full-time voluntary work. This may only be possible, however, if you have no commitments, as most of the work is away from home and you would have no means of supporting any dependants. Full-time volunteering has the advantage of giving you a sustained experience of what different kinds of work are really like and you will also be doing a useful job at the same time.

Few people can afford to support themselves while doing full-time voluntary work, so schemes have grown up which offer volunteers pocket money and free accommodation and board during the time they are working. This kind of work was pioneered and developed by an organisation called CSV (Community Service Volunteers) which places volunteers in full-time community service posts all over the UK.

It has its main office in London and local offices in other cities including Birmingham, Belfast, Glasgow and Cardiff. Each year CSV places over 2,500 volunteers in projects, making sure that people are sent to work where they are best suited. CSV organises its volunteers in two ways: through a central volunteer network, which is the way most volunteers work; and through a number of special schemes to encourage people who might not know about these volunteer opportunities. For example, through the Give and Take Scheme, people who are in care become volunteers, and Pre-Release Volunteering takes young people out of youth custody centres for the last month of their sentence to do full-time voluntary work.

CSV accepts anyone between the ages of 16 and 35 who really wants to do some community service, is willing to work away from home and is able to give a minimum of four months to the work. Placements are for a maximum period of one year. Volunteers need not have prior experience or any educational qualifications. No one is turned down. This policy of accepting everyone who wants to become a volunteer makes the interview a very important part of the work of CSV. Through the interview, people's strengths and weaknesses are discovered and discussed and decisions are made about possible kinds of work. No one is sent out on work which is likely to make impossible demands on them.

How to Apply

If you want to become a Community Service Volunteer you must write or call the London office (CSV, 237 Pentonville Road, London N1 9NJ; 0171 278 6601) for an application form. This form asks for your name, address, age and the names and addresses of two referees. You will then be asked to attend an interview at the CSV office nearest your home. At the interview you will want to answer all questions honestly, as the main point of the questions is to find out something about you and fit you into a placement to which you will be well suited and where you will be happy. Remember that nothing will exclude you from community service, even an episode about which you may be embarrassed, like a brush with the police. Or if, for example, you have had a period of psychiatric illness, it might simply mean that there are certain kinds of work which could place too much stress upon you and should be avoided.

As placements involve living away from home, free accommodation and board are provided. If no board is available, you will be given a weekly food allowance and provided with self-catering facilities. Your travelling expenses to and from the place of work at the beginning and end of your placement will be paid and you will get one week's holiday for every four months you work, again with the return fare to your home paid. You are also paid weekly pocket money and as a volunteer you do not pay any national insurance.

CSV places volunteers in face-to-face voluntary work with people in need: for example the elderly, disabled or homeless people, children in care or in trouble or people with mental illness or learning difficulties. There are opportunities to work with children and young people. Volunteers work in a variety of settings including hospitals, night shelters, day centres and group homes. Your placement will depend on what is available at the time you apply.

Advantages

The main advantages are in terms of the experience the work will give you. If you are a school-leaver, a year away from home will make you more mature, independent and able to cope with a job or with further education. If you are older and intend to change your career, you will want to be really sure that you are suited to the new work before embarking on training or a paid job. The sustained nature of CSV work allows you to discover if you can stand the pace, stress and demands of the job. In a very practical sense, you will fulfil the requirements of many training courses for a year's experience, you will make contacts who may be useful in supplying references when you make applications for training courses or jobs, and you may even find yourself a job as you could be asked to stay on as a paid employee at your volunteer placement.

Part 2

Introduction

There is no simple training formula for many of the jobs described in this book and there are often several routes which can be taken to the same job. However, certain factors crop up again and again. Entry requirements to many courses include work experience; academic entry requirements to the same course may vary from college to college or may, in the case of suitably experienced mature students, be waived.

Applying for a Place

The majority of courses in this field of work are full time and run by colleges of further education, but you will find courses offered on a day-release, block-release, sandwich and second-chance basis. Courses at colleges of further education begin in September, unless otherwise stated, and applications for a place should be made direct to the college of your choice at least 10 months before you wish to begin your studies.

A number of courses are run by institutions of higher education. Admissions to universities (for first degree courses) are handled by UCAS, the Universities and Colleges Admissions Service (see Useful Addresses). You can list up to eight courses and you should apply a year in advance. Applications to study for a higher degree should be made direct to the institutions concerned.

Where there are special application procedures, these have been set out separately.

Sources of Finance

Various kinds of grant are available from local education authorities (LEAs) in England and Wales or from the education authorities or Scottish Education Department in Scotland. You should enquire locally about these. Students embarking on postgraduate study may apply for grants to certain government departments, the Research Council, and other agencies. You can get further information from the Department for Education, Publication Centre, PO Box 2193, London E15 2EU (telephone 0181 533 2000) or from the Scottish Education Department, Awards Branch, Gyleview House, 3 Redheughs Rigg, Southgyle, Edinburgh EH12 9HH, or Department of Education, Scholarships Branch, Rathgael House, Balloo Road, Bangor, Co Down BT19 7PR. The DSS or Scottish Education Department may offer grants for postgraduate courses in social work. If you are taking a course as on-the-job training, you will continue to receive your salary while studying. If you want to take the course through a sponsorship scheme, you must first be accepted by the authority running the scheme and then you will be told what the application procedure is. You will be paid according to a set salary scale during your training.

Qualifications and Awards

There are a number of nationally recognised qualifications and awards which automatically entitle holders to salary increments. Before you enrol on a course leading to a college award, especially one offered by a private college, for which you will have to pay, be sure to find out whether or not the award is recognised and, if it is, by whom. If you are thinking of studying at a private college that does not have a national reputation, it is a good idea to look into the examination success rate and present employment of its ex-students.

Additional Information

Most of the information set out in Chapter 6 comes from primary sources, ie it was supplied by the professional or examining body concerned with the award and it was, to the best of our knowledge, correct at the time of writing, but you should check it with the institution whose course you want to take or the examining body for whose award you wish to study, as changes occur all the time. When you write for a prospectus or for information, send a large stamped and addressed envelope.

You should also consult the following annual publications which can be found in most public libraries: *British Qualifications* (Kogan Page), CRAC *Directory of Higher Education* (Hobson's Press), CRAC *Degree Course Guides* (Hobson's Press), *The Complete Degree Course Offers* and *Survey of HND Courses* (both from Trotman & Co Ltd, 12 Hill Rise, Richmond, Surrey TW10 6UA).

Background Reading

Adventure Playgrounds, an introduction (NPFA)
Careers in Social Work (Kogan Page)
Careers in Teaching (Kogan Page)
Children Under Stress (Pelican)
New Notes for Playleaders (PPA)
The Playgroup Movement (PPA)
Working with Children (Local Government Training Board)

Chapter 6

Qualifications, Awards and Courses

NURSERY NURSING AND WORK WITH YOUNG CHILDREN

Diploma of the NNEB

This nationally recognised award, given by the Council of Awards for Children's Care and Education (CACHE), is the leading provider of training in childcare for the 0–7 age group. (CACHE was formerly known as the NNEB; although the Council's name has changed, the qualification keeps the old name.) The Diploma in Nursery Nursing is awarded by the Board after two years up to a maximum of five years full-time or equivalent part-time training in childcare for the 0–7s. Currently about 270 courses are available at over 200 colleges in England, Wales, Northern Ireland and the Republic of Ireland and there is a growing demand from colleges to start new courses. The minimum age for admission to the course is 16, and there is no upper age limit. A number of non-standard courses have also been approved; these provide for a scheme of education and training over a somewhat longer period or training for students with special needs.

CACHE does not require applicants for the Diploma course to have GCSEs or any other academic award, but some colleges do demand three or more GCSE passes at grade A, B or C, and all operate a selection process. Courses usually start in September, but there are a few colleges where they start at other times in the year. Students apply direct to the college of their choice and, as courses are nearly always oversubscribed, should apply early. In college students follow an integrated course of vocational, social and complementary studies together with 140 days of practical workplace training. Sixty per cent of their time is spent in college, the rest in practical placements. The syllabus is divided into seven principal subject areas: observation and assessment; work with young children; cognitive and language development; child protection; the nursery nurse in employment; working with parents; early-years curriculum.

The Diploma is awarded to students who obtain a satisfactory grade for the continuous assessment of both college and practical work and who obtain a pass mark in the two papers of the final written examination. Students can only enter the examination in their final term of training. Those who fail the final examination are usually required to undergo a period of further training before they may resit, and no one may resit more than twice.

Students not ready to gain the Diploma can take the Preliminary Diploma in Nursery Nursing and upgrade to a full diploma after further training.

Some colleges offer Accreditation of Prior Learning (APL) systems which credit prior vocational experience so that the Diploma in Nursery Nursing can be achieved in less than two years. Courses which offer APL usually provide a mode of study designed for those already working in childcare so that students can study while continuing to work and these courses are therefore particularly relevant for mature women.

Colleges Offering the NNEB Diploma and Preliminary Diploma Course Listed under Local Authority

COUNTY COUNCILS
Avon (Bristol)
Bristol Nursery Nurses CFE, Weston-Super-Mare College, College of Care and Early Education

Bedfordshire
Dunstable C

Berkshire
Reading CT, East Berkshire C (Slough), Chiltern Nursery Training C (Reading), Norland Nursery Training C (Hungerford), Bracknell C

Birmingham
C of Food, Tourism and Creative Studies, East Birmingham C, Josiah Mason SFC (Erdington), North Birmingham C (Great Barr), South Birmingham C

Buckinghamshire
Amersham and Wycombe CFE, Aylesbury C, Milton Keynes C

Cambridgeshire
Cambridge Regional C, Peterborough Regional C

Cheshire
Halton CFE (Widnes), Mid-Cheshire CFE (Northwich), South Cheshire C (Crewe), Warrington Collegiate I, West Cheshire C (Chester), Stockport CFHE, Hyde Clarendon C, North Area C, Ridge Danvers C

Cleveland
Stockton-Billingham CFE, Hartlepool CFE

Clwyd
Emrys Ap Iwan, Yale C

Cornwall
Cornwall C (Falmouth), Saltash C

County Durham
Bishop Auckland C, Darlington CT, New College (Durham), Derwentside C (Consett), Newton Rigg C

Cumbria
Carlisle C, Furness C (Barrow In Furness), Kendal C, West Cumbria C (Workington)

Derbyshire
Mackworth C (Derby), North Derbyshire Tertiary C (Chesterfield), South East Derbyshire C (Ilkeston), Chesterfield CTA, High Peak C

Devon
Plymouth CFE, South Devon C (Torquay), North Devon C (Barnstaple), Combeshead C, Paignton C

Dorset
Bournemouth & Poole CFE (Poole), Weymouth C, The Dorchester (Thomas Hardy) S (Dorchester)

Dyfed
Carmarthenshire CT&A, Coleg Ceredigion (Aberystwyth), Pembrokeshire C (Haverfordwest)

Essex
Barking C, Colchester I, Thurrock C, Harlow C, Braintree C, Havering CHFE (Romford), Redbridge CFE (Romford), South East Essex CAT (Southend on Sea), Epping Forest C, Rainsford High S

Glamorgan (Mid, South, West)
Bridgend CT, Coleg Glan Hafran, Ystrad Mynach CFE, Swansea C, Pontypridd TC, Neath C, Merthyr Tydfil C, Rhondda C, Aberdare C, Aberdare Girls' S

Gloucestershire
Gloucester CAT (Cheltenham), Stroud CFE

Gwent
Gwent Tertiary C, Newport C, Pontypool Tertiary C

Gwynedd
Gwynedd TC (Bangor), Coleg Menai

Hampshire
Brockenhurst C, Basingstoke CT, Eastleigh C, Farnborough CT, Highbury CT (Portsmouth), St Vincent C, Fareham C, Southampton TC, Totton C

Hereford & Worcester
Herefordshire CT (Hereford), North East Worcestershire C

Hertfordshire
Hertford Regional C (Ware), Oaklands C (St Albans), West Herts C (Watford), St Albans Girls' S

Humberside
Grimsby CT, Hull C, North Lindsay C (Scunthorpe), Beverley CFE

Isle of Man
Isle of Man C (Douglas)

Isle of Wight
Isle of Wight C (Newport)

Jersey
Highlands C (Jersey)

Kent
Bexley C (Abbey Wood), Canterbury C, North West Kent CT (Gravesend), West Kent C (Tonbridge), Bromley CFHE, Canterbury High S

Lancashire
Accrington & Rossendale C, Blackpool and the Fylde C, Burnley C, Hopwood Hall C (Rochdale), Lancaster & Morecambe C, Maplesdon Noakes S (Maidstone), Nelson and Colne C, Preston C, Wigan and Leigh C, Oldham C, Blackburn C, Bolton C, Burnley C, Southport C, Cardinal Newman C

Leicestershire
South Fields C, Loughborough C

Lincolnshire
Grantham C, North Lincolnshire C (Lincoln), Stamford C, Boston C

Manchester
Bury C (Whitefield), Princess Christian C (Fallowfield), Salford C (Worsley), South Manchester C (Wythenshawe), South Trafford C (Altrincham), Tameside CT, City C, North Trafford C, Pendleton C

Merseyside
City of Liverpool Community C, Knowsley Community C (Southdene), St Helens C (Newton-le-Willows), Wirral Metropolitan C (Wallasey), Hugh Baird C

Middlesex
Ealing Tertiary C (Southall), Stanmore C, Enfield C, Richmond-upon-Thames C, Uxbridge C (Hayes), West Thames C (Isleworth), Feltham Community S, Spelthorne C

Midlands
Bilston Community C (Wolverhampton), Dudley CT, Sandwell CFHE (Smethwick), Solihull C, Sutton Coldfield CFE, Walsall CAT

Norfolk
Norfolk CAT (King's Lynn), Norwich City C

Northampton
Northampton C, Tresham Institute FHE

Northern Ireland
Antrim TC, Ballymena C, Belfast Institute FHE, East Tyrone FEC (Dungannon), Newry TC, North Down and Ards CFE (Holywood), North West Institute HE (Londonderry)

Northumberland
Northumberland CAT (Ashington)

Nottinghamshire
West Nottinghamshire C (Mansfield), Basford Hall CFE (Nottingham), Newark and Sherwood C, The Dukeries Community C

Oxfordshire
North Oxfordshire C (Banbury), Oxford C

Powys
Coleg Powys (Brecon)

Shropshire
Ludlow C, North Shropshire C, Shrewsbury CAT, Telford CAT

Somerset
Bridgwater C, Yeovil C, Somerset CAT, Strode C

Staffordshire
Burton-upon-Trent TC, Stoke on Trent C, Stafford C, Tamworth C

Suffolk
Suffolk C (Ipswich), Lowestoft C, West Suffolk C (Bury St Edmunds)

Surrey
Blackwater Valley Centre (Camberley), Carshalton C, Croydon C, Guildford CFHE, East Surrey C (Redhill), Kingston C, Merton C, North East Surrey CT (Ewell), Godalming C, Woking C

Sussex (East and West)
Bexhill C, Brighton C, Chichester CAST, Crawley C, Eastbourne CAT, Northbrook C, C of Richard Collyer

Tyne & Wear
Gateshead C, Monkwearmouth C, Newcastle C, North Tyneside C (North Shields), South Tyneside C (South Shields), Tynemouth C

Warwickshire
Mid-Warwickshire C (Leamington Spa), North Warwickshire CAT (Nuneaton), Rugby CFE, Tile Hill FEC (Coventry)

Wiltshire
Swindon C

Worcestershire
Evesham C, North East Worcestershire C (Bromsgrove), Worcester Sixth Form C

Yorkshire
Calderdale C (Halifax), Dewsbury C, Harrogate C, Huddersfield TC, Keighley C, York CAT, Barnsley C, Bradford & Ilkley Community C (Bradford), Craven C (Skipton), Doncaster C, Rother Valley C (Sheffield),

Sheffield C, Thomas Danby C (Leeds), Wakefield C (Hemsworth), Yorkshire Coast CFHE (Scarborough)

LONDON
Barnet C, City of Westminster C, C of North East London (Tottenham), Hackney Community C, Agency for Jewish Education, Ealing Tertiary C, Kensington & Chelsea C, Lambeth C (Brixton), Leyton Sixth Form C, London Montessori Centre, Negus Sixth Form S (Plumstead), Newham Community C (Stratford), City & Islington C, C of North West London, St Francis Xavier (Wandsworth), Southwark C, Tower Hamlets C, Waltham Forest C

Colleges Offering Non-standard NNEB Courses
THREE-YEAR PART-TIME COURSES
Check with your local college to see if it will offer part-time courses. Colleges will often do so, perhaps starting in February, if they have had enough requests to make a part-time course viable.

COURSES FOR DEAF STUDENTS
Basford Hall CFE

WELSH BI-LINGUAL COURSES
Some of the colleges in Wales offer bilingual courses: Bridgend CT, Carmarthenshire CT & A, Gwynedd TC, NE Wales I.

PRIVATE COLLEGES
Chiltern Nursery Training C (Reading), London Montessori Centre, Norland Nursery TC (Hungerford), The Princess Christian C (Fallowfield, Manchester)

Most of these colleges are residential and charge fees.

The NNEB Diploma in Post-Qualifying Studies (DPQS)

The DPQS courses on offer by colleges vary quite substantially since the curriculum for each course is, in large measure, defined by an individual college. Each college will provide details of the units available and the dates, times and places where training may be obtained.

There are no formal entry requirements for the DPQS but prospective candidates must have had at least two years' professional practice in the care of children aged 0 to 8, either full time or part-time equivalent, in a daycare, health or education environment. Candidates will need to demonstrate they have the ability to benefit from and contribute to the course of study; candidates with little or no academic background may have difficulty in undertaking the award.

Candidates will also need to provide evidence of knowledge in areas of child development and education such as physical care and development, emotional and social development, cognitive and language development, working with parents, work with babies and early-years curriculum.

A course normally covers two years of part-time study, mostly on a day-release basis, but there is no requirement to complete it in this time scale. There are six units of study, which may be taken one at a time and not necessarily consecutively. Each unit has 60 classroom and 60 practical hours. The course's structure is three units of 'child and family studies', two units of 'professional, management and the context of services' and a sixth unit consisting of one term's in-depth study of a subject of the student's choice related to child care.

Application should be made direct to the college; funding is sometimes undertaken by employers.

The Open University course P554 Child Abuse and Neglect can be accredited as one unit towards the DPQS, provided that the candidate registers with CACHE and passes an assignment set by the Council before beginning the OU course.

Colleges Offering the NNEB DPQS Listed under Local Authority

COUNTY COUNCILS

Bedfordshire
Dunstable C

Berkshire
Reading CT, Chiltern Nursery Training C (Reading)

Cambridgeshire
Peterborough Regional C

Devon
South Devon CAT

Essex
Havering CFHE (Romford)

Hampshire
Basingstoke CT, Highbury CT (Portsmouth)

Hertfordshire
Hertford Regional C (Ware), Oaklands C (City Campus, St Albans)

Humberside
North Lindsey C (Scunthorpe)

Nottinghamshire
Basford Hall C (Nottingham)

Staffordshire
Stoke-on-Trent C, Tamworth C

Suffolk
Suffolk C (Ipswich)

Surrey
Croydon C

Yorkshire
Dewsbury C

METROPOLITAN DISTRICTS

Birmingham
Birmingham CET

Durham
New C Durham

Manchester
Bury Metropolitan C, South Trafford C (Altrincham)

North Tyneside
North Tyneside C (North Shields)

Preston
Preston C

St Helens
St Helens C (Newton-le-Willows)

Sandwell
Sandwell CFHE (Smethwick Sandwell)

Sheffield
Rother Valley C

Stockport
Stockport CFHE

Wakefield
Wakefield C

Walsall
Walsall CAT

Wirral
Wirral Metropolitan C

LONDON

City & Islington C, College of NW London, Croydon C, Lambeth C, Southwark C, Uxbridge C, Waltham Forest C

NVQ (National Vocational Qualification)

NVQs in Child Care and Education (Work in a Community Run Group), Child Care and Education (Work with Babies), Child Care and Education (Work in a Pre-School Group), and Child Care and

Education (Work in Support of Others) awarded by BTEC or CACHE or JAB are validated at Level 2.

NVQs in Child Care and Education (Group Care and Education), Child Care and Education (Family Day Care), and Child Care and Education (Pre-School Provision) awarded by BTEC or CACHE or JAB are validated at Level 3.

NVQs in Playwork awarded by City & Guilds are validated at Level 2 and Level 3.

NVQs in Playwork Development awarded by City & Guilds are validated at Level 4.

The NNEB Diploma is equal to at least NVQ Level 2.

APEL (Accreditation of Prior Experience and Learning)

APEL allows a candidate's previous experience and learning to be assessed and accredited to him or her. This can allow remission from certain aspects of the college curriculum, so that candidates can achieve their qualification without needing to attend college full time. Not all colleges have an APEL scheme, so students should first check with the college that it will be using APEL to credit NNEB awards. Evidence of prior learning can be given as certificates, references and letters, and includes voluntary work authenticated by a responsible person.

Scottish Nursery Nurses' Board (SNNB)

To qualify for registration with the SNNB, nursery nurses must have successfully completed a two-year course of relevant SCOTVEC National Certificate modules. Students spend the equivalent of two days per week in college and at least 140 days altogether in practical training at a nursery school, day nursery, children's or family centre or infant department in a primary school.

SCOTVEC NC modules approved by the Board are given below; some exemptions may be given, for instance, for a Standard First Aid Certificate, O Grade Home Economics, and Standard Grade passes at Band 1, 2 or 3 in appropriate subjects.

96003	First aid measures
96053	Prevention of infection
76065	Language development: Children 0–8 years (×2)
86066	Music and the young child 0–8 years (×3)
76067	Poetry storytelling and the development of the child 0–8 years (×3)
76068	Play and the development of the child 0–8 years (×4)
76069	The young child and discovery of the environment (×3)
76070	The family, the community and the child 0–8 years (×2)
86071	Children's clothing and nursery equipment (×2)

76088	Art and crafts in the development of the child 0–8 years (×2)
7140330	Child health (×2)
7140350	Preparation for a child's admission to and discharge from hospital (×½)
7140360	Care of the sick child (×½)
7140860	Human development: Birth to 8 years (×4)
7150520	Nutrition and menu planning
7150610	Practical fabric skills

Colleges Offering Programmes of Study
Aberdeen CFE, Borders C, Clackmannan CFE, Clydebank C, Coatbridge C, Dumfries and Galloway CT, Dundee C, Falkirk CT, Fife CT, Glasgow C of Nautical Studies; Inverness C, James Watt C, Jewel and Esk Valley C, Kilmarnock C, Langside C, Lauder C, Moray CFE, Motherwell C, Stevenson C, Thurso C, West Lothian C.

SNNB Post-Certificate Award in Nursing

The one-year course is run on a day-release basis. It expands the nursery nurse's theoretical knowledge and gives some instruction in management techniques. Applicants should hold the SNNB Certificate and have had three years' approved experience.

Colleges Running SNNB Post-Certificate Award Courses
Dundee CCom, Esk Valley C, Falkirk CT, Kirkcaldy CT, Lauder C (Dunfermline), West Lothian CFE.

For details write to the SNNB (see Useful Addresses).

Private Nursery Training Colleges

The colleges listed below charge fees and specialise in preparing students for private posts. Their two-year or 18-month residential courses cover the care of children from birth to the age of seven. They combine in-college vocational and general studies with practical training in a variety of settings and include experience of child care during 24 hours of the day. The courses lead to the NNEB Diploma and Preliminary Diploma or SNNB registration and to a recognised college certificate. Successful candidates can go on to take the examination for the Royal Society of Health diploma.

Chiltern Nursery Training College, 20 and 32 Peppard Road, Caversham, Reading, Berkshire RG4 8JZ
London Montessori Centre, 18 Balderton Street, London W1Y 1TG (non-residential)
Norland Nursery Training College, Denford Park, Hungerford, Berkshire, RG17 0PQ

The Princess Christian College, 26 Wilbraham Road, Fallowfield, Manchester M14 6JX

Business & Technology Education Council (BTEC)

BTEC National Certificates (NC) and Diplomas (ND) in the Caring Services (Nursery Nursing) courses are approved to run at the following colleges:

Avon (Bristol)
Brunel CAT (Bristol), ND; College of Care and Early Education (Bristol), ND; Norton-Radstock C (Bath), ND; Weston-Super-Mare C, ND

Barnet
Barnet C, ND; Hendon C (London), ND

Bedfordshire
Bedford CHE, NC, ND; Dunstable C, NC, ND

Birmingham
Bournville CFE, NC, ND; East Birmingham C, NC, ND; Handsworth C, NC, ND; Joseph Chamberlain C, ND; South Birmingham C, NC, ND; Sutton Coldfield CFE, NC, ND

Bolton
Bolton C, NC, ND

Bradford
Bradford & Ilkley CC, NC, ND; Keighley C, NC, ND; Shipley C, NC, ND

Bromley
Orpington CFE, ND

Buckinghamshire
Amersham & Wycombe C, ND

Cambridgeshire
Cambridge Regional C, NC, ND; Isle C (Wisbech), NC, ND; Peterborough Regional C, NC, ND

Cheshire
Macclesfield CFE, NC, ND; Mid-Cheshire CFE (Northwich), ND; Warrington Collegiate Institute, NC, ND

Cleveland
Middlesbrough CFE, NC, ND; Stockton & Billingham C, NC, ND

Clwyd
Deeside C, ND; Landrillo TC (Colwyn Bay), ND; Yale C (Wrexham), NC, ND

Cornwall
Cornwall C (Redruth), NC, ND; Penwith C (Penzance), NC, ND; St Austell C, ND

Coventry
Coventry TC, NC, ND; Tile Hill CFE, NC, ND

Cumbria
Kendal C, NC, ND

Derbyshire
Derby Tertiary C (Wilmorton), NC, ND; High Peak C (Buxton), NC; Mackworth C (Derby), ND; North Derbyshire TC (Chesterfield), NC, ND; South East Derbyshire C (Ilkeston), ND

Devon
East Devon C (Tiverton), ND; Exeter C, NC, ND; Exmouth Community C, ND; N Devon C, NC; S Devon C (Torquay), ND; Tavistock C, ND; Teignmouth CC, NC, ND

Doncaster
Doncaster C, ND

Dorset
Bournemouth & Poole CFE, ND

Dudley
Stourbridge C, ND

Durham
Darlington CT, NC, ND; Peterlee C, NC, ND; St Bede's RC S (Peterlee), ND

Dyfed
Carmarthenshire CTA (Llanelli), ND; Coleg Ceredigion (Aberystwyth), ND

Ealing
Ealing TC (Southhall), ND

East Sussex
Bexhill C, NC, ND; Brighton CT, ND; Eastbourne CAT, ND; Hastings CAT, ND

Enfield
Enfield C, ND

Essex
Basildon C, ND; Braintree C, ND; Chelmsford C, NC, ND; Colchester I, ND; Epping Forest C (Loughton), NC, ND; South East Essex C, NC, ND; Thurrock C (Grays), ND

Gateshead
Gateshead C, NC, ND

Gwent
Gwent TC (Usk), ND

Gwynedd
Coleg Meirion Dwyfor (Dolgellau), NC, ND; Coleg Menai (Bangor), ND

Hackney
Hackney CC (London), NC, ND

Hammersmith
Hammersmith & West London C, NC, ND

Hampshire
Alton C, ND; Basingstoke CT, ND; Eastleigh C, ND; Fareham C, ND; Highbury CT (Portsmouth), ND; Southampton TC, NC, ND; South Downs C, ND

Harrow
Elm Park C (Stanmore), NC, ND

Hereford and Worcester
Worcester CT, ND

Hertfordshire
North Hertfordshire C (Stevenage), NC, ND

Hounslow
West Thames C (Isleworth), ND

Humberside
East Yorkshire CFE (Bridlington), ND; Hull C, NC, ND

Isle of Wight
Isle of Wight C (Newport), ND

Kent
Canterbury C, ND; Mid-Kent CHFE (Chatham), NC, ND; North West Kent CT (Dartford), NC, ND; South Kent C (Folkestone), NC, ND; Thanet C (Broadstairs), NC, ND; West Kent C (Tonbridge), NC, ND

Kirklees
Dewsbury C, NC, ND

Lambeth
Lambeth C (London), NC, ND

Lancashire
Accrington & Rossendale C, NC, ND; Blackburn C, NC, ND; Blackpool & The Fylde C, NC; Burnley C, ND; Lancaster & Morecambe C, ND; Preston C, NC, ND; Runshaw C, NC, ND; Skelmersdale C, NC, ND; St Mary's C, NC, ND

Leeds
Airedale & Wharfedale C, NC, ND; Park Lane C, NC, ND; Thomas Danby C (Leeds), NC, ND

Leicestershire
Coalville TC (Leicester), ND; Leicester South Fields C, ND; Melton Mowbray CFE, NC, ND; Our Lady's Convent S (Loughborough), ND; Rutland C, ND; Wigston CFE, ND

Lewisham
Lewisham C (London), ND

Lincolnshire
Boston C, NC, ND; North Lincolnshire C, ND

Liverpool
Liverpool CC, ND

Manchester
City C, ND

Mid Glamorgan
Merthyr Tydfil C, NC, ND; Pontypridd TC, ND; Ystrad Mynach C (Hengoed), ND

Newcastle
Newcastle C, ND

Norfolk
Great Yarmouth CFE, ND; Norwich City C, NC, ND

North Tyneside
North Tyneside C (Wallsend), NC, ND

North Yorkshire
Selby C, NC, ND; York CFHE, NC, ND

Northamptonshire
Daventry TC, NC, ND; Northampton C, NC, ND

Northumberland
Northumberland CAT (Ashington), ND

Nottinghamshire
Basford Hall C (Nottingham), ND; Broxtowe C (Beeston), ND

Oldham
Oldham C, NC, ND

Oxfordshire
Abingdon C, ND; Henley C (Henley-on-Thames), ND; West Oxfordshire C (Witney), NC, ND

Powys
Coleg Powys (Newtown), NC, ND

Rochdale
Hopwood Hall C (Middleton), NC, ND

Rotherham
Rockingham CFE (Rotherham), NC, ND; Rotherham CAT, ND

Salford
Salford C (Manchester), NC, ND

Sandwell
Sandwell CFHE, ND

Sefton
Hugh Baird C (Bootle), NC, ND; Southport C, NC, ND

Sheffield
Sheffield C, NC

Shropshire
Shrewsbury CAT, ND; Telford CAT, ND

Solihull
Archbishop Grimshaw S (Birmingham), ND; Kingshurst CTC (Birmingham), ND; Solihull C, NC, ND

Somerset
Bridgwater C, NC, ND; Somerset CAT (Taunton), NC, ND; Strode C, NC, ND

South Glamorgan
Barry C, ND; Coleg Glan Hafren (Cardiff), ND

South Tyneside
South Tyneside C (South Shields), ND

Southwark
Southwark C (London), ND

Staffordshire
Cannock Chase TC, ND; Leek CFE, ND; Stafford C, ND

Stockport
Stockport CFHE, NC, ND; North Area C, NC, ND

Suffolk
Lowestoft C, NC, ND; Suffolk C (Ipswich), NC, ND; West Suffolk C (Bury St Edmunds), NC, ND

Surrey
Guildford CFHE, ND

Tameside
Tameside CT (Ashton-under-Lyne), ND

Trafford
North Trafford CFE (Manchester), NC, ND

Walsall
Walsall CAT, NC, ND

Wandsworth
South Thames C (London), NC, ND

West Glamorgan
Gorseinon C, NC, ND; Swansea C, ND

West Sussex
Chichester C, ND; Northbrook C (Worthing), NC, ND

Wigan
Wigan & Leigh C, ND

Wiltshire
New C (Swindon), NC, ND; Salisbury C, NC, ND; Trowbridge C, NC, ND

Wolverhampton
Bilston CC (Wolverhampton), NC, ND; Wulfrun C (Wolverhampton), NC, ND

NORTHERN IRELAND

North-Eastern Area
Causeway IFHE NC, ND; Antrim IFHE NC, ND

South-Eastern Area
Castlereagh CFE (Belfast), NC, ND; East Down IFHE NC, ND; North Down and Ards C, ND

Scottish Vocational Education Council (SCOTVEC)

SCOTVEC National Certificate modules relevant to Nursery Nursing are offered by the following colleges:

Aberdeen, Borders, Clackmannan, Clydebank, Coatbridge, Falkirk, Glasgow, Glasgow C of Nautical Studies, Inverness, James Watt, Jewel and Usk Valley, Kilmarnock, Lauder, Moray, Motherwell, Stevenson, Thurso

Colleges offering the SCOTVEC HNC Working with Children in Their Early Years:

Clydebank C, Dundee CFE, Falkirk CT, Fife CT, James Watt C, Langside C, Motherwell C, Perth CFE.

Miscellaneous College Awards in Nursery Nursing

Certificate in Child Care; Certificate in Child Development – Basingstoke CT, Blackpool and the Fylde C, Central Lancashire C, Stoke-on-Trent C, West Kent C
Certificate in Child Minding – Isle C, Tile Hill CFE (Coventry); Stafford C
Certificate for Nursery Aides – Exeter C

Playgroup Courses: The Pre-school Playgroups Association (PPA)

England
The PPA runs Diploma, Basic and many other types of course, from one-day workshops to one-day-a-week courses lasting one or two years. These courses are designed to help anyone who has dealings with children under five and particularly to equip students to work in a playgroup.

Most courses take place at adult education centres and colleges of further education, some of which may have a playgroup or crèche attached to them. The courses are open to anyone interested in under-fives. Fees vary widely, but in some areas considerable reductions are offered to people receiving family income supplement or supplementary benefit.

There is a tutor assigned to each course and students are encouraged to negotiate course content. The course generally takes the form of discussions on a variety of subjects concerning under-fives together with practical sessions within the course and at playgroups. Visiting speakers are invited to talk on special topics. The emphasis is on the development of the young child within the family and playgroup and the value of play as an aid to early education. Practical advice on the setting up and running of a playgroup is also given.

Courses are held in all parts of England and are too numerous for there to be a single list. Your local PPA organiser will give you details of those in your area or you can write to the PPA head office (see Useful Addresses).

Diploma in Playgroup Practice

The Diploma conforms with the Guidance to the Children Act 1989, which requires that in a playgroup 'at least half the staff should hold a relevant qualification in day care or education, or have completed a training course specified by the Pre-school Playgroups Association (PPA) or other voluntary body'.

The course covers the theoretical knowledge and practical skills needed in organising and administering a playgroup or nursery, and provides the underpinning knowledge and understanding needed for the NVQ in Child Care and Education Levels 2 or 3. The course consists of 150 to 160 hours' class contact time plus 40 to 50 hours' student assignments. Students must have access to or be working (paid or unpaid) in a playgroup or nursery.

Basic Course Learning Through Play

The course provides a basic knowledge and understanding of the development and education of children under statutory school age and demonstrates how to provide quality care and education for children under five in playgroup and nursery, and in the home. It lasts 20 to 24 class contact hours and is linked to the NVQ.

Scotland, Wales and Northern Ireland
Scotland, Wales and Northern Ireland each has its own autonomous association which organises courses. Write to the Glasgow, Clwyd or Belfast office for the addresses of local contacts.

CARE WORK

City and Guilds of London Institute (C&G)

C&G, Britain's largest testing and awarding body in technical and vocational education and training, offers a number of schemes leading to qualifications in caring. Courses are run in many colleges of further education throughout the UK.

Caring for Children 0–7 years (3240); C&G Level 2
Usually a part-time or in-service course for students aged 18 or over.

Family and Community Care (3310); C&G Level 2
Normally a two-year full-time course for 16- to 18-year-olds but may be shorter for mature students.

Practical Caring Skills (3560); Parts I and II; C&G Levels 1 and 2
A two-part scheme primarily for YT trainees in care placements.

Community Care Practice (3250); C&G Level 2
Usually a part-time or in-service course for students aged 18 and over.

Foundation Management for Care (3250); C&G Level 3
A scheme for those who hold or hope to take up a supervisory post in care. Minimum age for students normally 20 and over.

Advanced Management for Care (3250) (Career Extension)
For senior staff and management in care.

Holders of certificates for the 3250 scheme work in a wide range of jobs with young and elderly people as well as people with special needs, in the public, private and voluntary sectors. An increasing number of people are progressing to further training after gaining work experience. Each of these schemes allows progression to Foundation and Advanced Management for Care (3250). For further information including a list of centres offering courses, please contact C&G (see Useful Addresses).

Business & Technology Education Council (BTEC)

BTEC's awards are nationally recognised; relevant courses, run in many colleges of further education throughout England, Wales and Northern Ireland, are:

First Certificate in Caring

First Diploma in Caring

National Certificate in Caring Services (Social Care)

National Diploma in Caring Services (Social Care)

National Certificate in Science (Health Studies)

National Diploma in Science (Health Studies)

GNVQ Level 2 (Health and Social Care)

GNVQ Level 3 (Health and Social Care)

For details and a list of centres offering courses, please contact BTEC (see Useful Addresses).

Scottish Vocational Education Council (SCOTVEC)

SCOTVEC is responsible for developing, administering and assessing the National Certificate. The award is available in a variety of modes of study in schools, colleges and other approved centres. It may be taken, for example: alongside, or as an extension to, Standard Grade, Higher Grade or Certificate of Sixth Year Studies in the fifth and sixth years of secondary education; on a full- or part-time basis in a college of further education; on a consortium basis with part of the programme being provided by a school and part by a college or part by a college and part by another approved centre; as part of a TVEI scheme; as part of a YT scheme; by adults seeking new skills or retraining. Programmes are made up of modules, ie units of study, and most modules are based upon a nominal 40 hours' teaching and learning.

Module descriptors

D7 Social and Welfare Work

66134	Basic general factors in the health of children and young people
76013	Family structure and roles
66043	Human development: severe and profound mentally handicapped children (×2)
7140840	Human development: the adolescent
71480	Introduction to youth work
66018	Practical caring skills: adolescents (×3)

D8 Education & Training

76088	Art and crafts in the development of the child 0–8 years (×2)
61523	Care of babies and young children in the home
96103	Family and pre-school partnerships
7140860	Human development: birth to 8 years (×4)
96026	Human development: 0–puberty
90011	Introduction to the role of movement in human development
7140800	Introduction to human development: infancy to old age
76065	Language development: children 0–8 years (×2)
86066	Music and the young child 0–8 years (×2)
76075	Nursery organisation (×2)
76068	Play and the development of the child 0–8 years (×4)
86077	Playground organisation

76067   Poetry and storytelling in the development of the child 0-8 years (×3)

7260061   The organisation of the care and education environment for children under 8 (×2)

96081   The role of movement in the development of the child 0-8 years

76069   The young child and discovery of the environment (×3)

H3 Home Economics

86071   Children's clothing and nursery equipment

7150520   Nutrition and menu planning

7150610   Practical fabric skills

M6 Nursing

7140360   Care of the sick child (×1½)

7140330   Child health (×2)

76016   Practical caring skills: the young child

66001   Practical caring skills 1 (×3)

7140350   Preparation for a child's admission to and discharge from hospital (×½)

M9 Personal Health Care and Fitness

96003   First aid measures

Note: Figures in brackets refer to multiples or fractions of modules. A module normally lasts 40 hours.

SCOTVEC also validates a Higher National Certificate in Working with Children in their Early Years. This award is available at the following Colleges: Clydebank C, Dundee CFE, Falkirk CT, James Watt C, Langside C, Fife CT, Moray CFE, Motherwell C, Perth CFE.

Other Awards

The National Association for Maternal and Child Welfare (NAMCW) offers a Certificate in Human Development and Family Life at: Basford Hall CFE, Brighton CT, Cambridge Regional C, Chichester C, Chippenham C, Dunstable C, Eastbourne CAT, Grimsby C, Melton Mowbray CFE, North East Worcestershire C, North Lincolnshire C, Peterborough Regional C, Plymouth CFE, Portsmouth C, Sandwell CFHE, Stockport CFHE, Taunton C, West Kent C.

NAMCW offers a Diploma in Human Development, Child Care and Social Responsibility at: Burton upon Trent TC, Cannock Chase TC, Chippenham C, Derby Tertiary C, Dunstable C, Farnborough SFC, Grimsby C, Melton Mowbray CFE, North East Worcestershire C, North Lincolnshire C, North Lindsey C, North West Kent CT, Portsmouth C, Queen Mary's C, South Cheshire C, South Kent C, Tameside CT, Taunton C, West Kent C, Worcester SPC.

Certificate in School Nursing is available at the following colleges: Brighton,

Central England in Birmingham, Croydon, East London, Hertfordshire, Nene, New C (Durham), North E Surrey CT, Suffolk, Wolverhampton.

CACHE offers a bilingual (Welsh/English) Certificate in Children's Care and Education at: Bridgend CT, Carmarthenshire CTA, Gwynedd TC, North East Wales I.

The following colleges offer a certificate/diploma for nursery nurses: Darlington CT, Stoke on Trent C, Telford CAT.

There is a certificate/diploma for nursery aides at Exeter C.

Access in nursery nursing is offered at: Birmingham C Food Tourism & Creative Studies, City of Liverpool Community C, Sutton Coldfield CFE.

Child Care courses are offered at: Barking CT, Brighton CT, Hertford Regional C, Handsworth C, Parkwood (Sheffield), Rockingham CFE, St Helens C, South Cheshire C, South Kent C, Stevenson C (Edinburgh), Stockton & Billingham CFE, Swindon C, Wakefield C, Wirral Metropolitan C.

Child development through play is available at: Eastbourne CAT, Newark & Sherwood C, St Helens C.

There is a course for child minders at: Barnfield C (Luton), Carmarthenshire CTA, East Birmingham C, Handsworth C, Rother Valley C, Wirral Metropolitan C.

SOCIAL WORK

The Central Council for Education and Training in Social Work (CCETSW)

The CCETSW has statutory responsibility for promoting and recognising courses for training in all fields of social work, including residential and day services. The single qualifying award in social work, the Diploma in Social Work (DipSW), awarded by the CCETSW, is now the only professional qualification.

National Vocational Qualifications (NVQs) in Care are awarded by CCETSW and City & Guilds; Scottish Vocational Qualifications (SVQs) in Care are awarded jointly by the Scottish Vocational Education Council (SCOTVEC) and CCETSW. They are open to full-time, part-time, waged earners and the unwaged.

The NVQ awards in Child Care and Education listed below are offered by CCETSW in England, Wales and Northern Ireland. (In Scotland the SVQs are offered only by SCOTVEC.)

Level 2
Q101 1110　Work with babies
Q101 1111　Work in support of others
Q101 1107　Work in a pre-school group
Q101 1104　Work in a community-run pre-school playgroup

Level 3
Q101 1106   Group care and education
Q101 1105   Family day care
Q101 1108   Pre-school provision

It is not always necessary to obtain vocational qualifications to reach the qualifying level in social work. Many people go straight into qualifying level, though normally they will have had some experience of work, either paid or voluntary, in the social services.

DipSW (Diploma in Social Work)

There are two main routes to the Diploma in Social Work: employment based and college based. College-based students are normally on full-time college courses, which are known as programmes. Early application is advised. Application forms are available from the Social Work Admissions System (SWAS), Fulton House, Jessop Avenue, Cheltenham, Gloucestershire GL50 3SH or from CCETSW offices in London, Edinburgh, Cardiff and Belfast; applications should be made by 15 December. Most non-graduate and post-graduate college-based programmes recruit through SWAS. Undergraduate programmes (courses) recruit through the Universities and Colleges Admission Service (UCAS) (see Useful Addresses).

Candidates under the age of 21 when they begin the DipSW programme must have either two A-level passes at grade A, B, C, D or E and GCSE passes grade A, B or C, in three other subjects; or five SCE passes including three at the Higher Level; or equivalent qualifications. Candidates aged 21 and over do not need formal educational qualifications but must satisfy colleges of their ability to study at advanced level.

Employment-based students are nominated by their social service employers and continue in their job, combining academic study with job practice.

All DipSW students train for at least two years (study and supervised practice) unless they already hold formally endorsed credits of assessed academic study incorporating acceptable relevant practice learning.

For qualified staff there are courses of post-qualifying study approved by CCETSW, with two new awards: the Post Qualifying Award (CCETSW) and the Advanced Award.

Students can also take the Diploma of Higher Education in Social Work.

College-based DipSW programmes, colleges and programme co-ordinators

NORTHERN ENGLAND
Merseyside Training Partnership, Wirral Social Services Dept, Birkenhead; U of Liverpool; Bradford U; U of Durham; New C Durham; U of Sunderland; U of Huddersfield; U of Humberside; U of Hull; Bradford & Ilkley C; U of Lancaster; Leeds Metropolitan U; Manchester U; Manchester Metropolitan U; U of Teesside; U of Northumbria at Newcastle; U of Central Lancashire; UC Salford; Sheffield Hallam U; Sheffield U; Stockport CFHE; Bretton Hall C, Wakefield; Goodricke C, U of York

SOUTH-EAST ENGLAND AND LONDON BOROUGHS
U of Sussex; Canterbury Christ Church C; Keynes C, U of Kent at Canterbury; Mid-Kent CHFE, Chatham; Middlesex U; Havering CFHE; U of East London; U of North London; Royal Holloway C, U of London; South Bank U; Bromley CFHE; West London IHE

SOUTH-WEST ENGLAND
U of Bath; U of the West of England, Bristol; Bristol U; Cheltenham & Gloucester CHE; U of Exeter; U of Plymouth; East Devon C; U of Portsmouth; Cornwall C; U of Southampton; Trowbridge C

WELSH BORDERS TO EAST ANGLIA
Birmingham and W Midlands DipSW Partnership; Bourneville CFE; Selly Oak C; U of Birmingham; North East Worcestershire C; Anglia Polytechnic U; Buckinghamshire CHE; Coventry U; U of Warwick; U of Derby; U of Wolverhampton; U of Hertfordshire; Suffolk C; Keele U; De Montfort U; U of Leicester; Luton CHE; Nene C; City C Norwich; U of East Anglia; Nottingham Trent U; U of Nottingham; U of Oxford; Oxford Brookes U; Ruskin C; U of Reading; West Herts C; Staffordshire U

NORTHERN IRELAND
Belfast I FHE

SCOTLAND
The Robert Gordon U, Aberdeen; Northern C, Aberdeen Campus; U of Dundee; Northern C, Dundee Campus; Moray House C, Edinburgh; U of Strathclyde; Glasgow Caledonian U; U of Glasgow; U of Stirling

WALES
U C of North Wales, Bangor; Gwynedd TC; North East Wales I; U of Wales C of Cardiff

Courses for undergraduates
Some institutions of higher education offer four-year degree courses, or programmes, as they are called, recognised by the CCETSW as leading to the DipSW. The degree is usually in social science or sociology and social work combined with different options, one of which leads to the professional social work

qualification. You need to satisfy degree-course entry requirements for these courses.

Institutions offering degree courses

Bath U; Central England in Birmingham U; Bradford U; Buckinghamshire CHE; Strathclyde U; Paisley U; Hertfordshire U; Hull U; Lancaster U; Middlesex U; South Bank U; North London U; Ulster U; Manchester Metropolitan U; Plymouth U; Central Lancashire U; Reading U; Redruth C, Cornwall; University C, Salford; Sheffield Hallam U; Southampton U; Stirling U

Institutions offering two-year DipHE courses

The Robert Gordon U, Aberdeen; Coventry U; Havering CFHE; Liverpool U; New College Durham; Sutherland U; Huddersfield U; Humberside U; Bradford & Ilkley C; Leeds Metropolitan U; Manchester U; Teesside U; University of Northumbria at Newcastle; Central Lancashire U; University College Salford; Sheffield Hallam U; Bretton Hall C; Sussex U; Canterbury Christ Church C; Mid-Kent CHFE; Southampton U; Oxford Brookes U; Havering C; East London U; North London U; Greenwich U; Brunel U; Bristol U; Cheltenham & Gloucester CHE; Plymouth U; East Devon C; Bournemouth U; Portsmouth U; Cornwall C; Southampton IHE; Trowbridge C; U of Central England in Birmingham; Bourneville CFE; Selly Oak C; North East Worcestershire C, Bromsgrove; Anglia Polytechnic U; Buckinghamshire CHE; Coventry U; Derby U; Wolverhampton U; Suffolk C; De Montfort U, Leicester and Milton Keynes; Luton CHE; City C Norwich; Nottingham Trent U; Oxford Brookes U; Bracknell C; West Herts C, Watford; Staffordshire U; Ulster U at Jordanstown; U C of North Wales, Bangor

Institutions offering postgraduate courses

Glasgow U; Liverpool U; Durham U; Lancaster U; Manchester U; Central Lancashire U; Sheffield U; York U; Sussex U; U of Kent at Canterbury; Goldsmiths C; Kingston U; London School of Economics; Middlesex U; London U; South Bank U; Brunel U; Bristol U; Southampton U; Birmingham U; Warwick U; Keele U; Leicester U; U of East Anglia, Norwich; Nottingham U; U Oxford; Queen's U of Belfast; Ulster U; The Robert Gordon U, Aberdeen; Northern C; Dundee U; Edinburgh U; Stirling U; Gwynedd TC; North East Wales I; Tavistock Clinic, London; I of Family Therapy, London

Courses for people with family commitments

A few programmes are provided for those whose family commitments prevent their taking the regular courses. The course content is the same as on the other CQSW courses but the college day and practice placements are shorter and there may be longer holidays.

CATS and APEL

Some courses, or programmes, allow credits to give exemption from part of the course. If the credits have been gained through a framework of organised education and training, the system is known as CATS (credit accumulation and transfer system); if the credits have been gained through relevant experience, the system is called APEL (assessment through prior assessment and learning).

Full details of CATS, APEL, part-time and family-responsibility courses are included in the CCETSW handbook *How to Qualify for Social Work,* which lists all employment-based and college-based programmes in detail.

Post-Qualifying Awards

CCETSW Post-Qualifying and Advanced Awards are awarded through a framework of continuing professional development. The framework takes staff from the point of professional qualification (DipSW) to post-qualifying level and on to advanced level – where they provide leadership and expertise.

The framework consists of six components:

- CATS (see above) linked to academic awards
- Post-qualifying and advanced levels of professional development leading to CCETSW awards
- Assessment of learning results
- Implementation through consortia of agencies and education institutions
- A monitoring system
- A UK-wide standard of education and training established and maintained by CCETSW.

Candidates can accumulate credits by demonstrating a competence to a standard recognised by CCETSW. Up to 120 credits can be accumulated at post-qualifying level, equivalent to the academic level of the final year of an undergraduate degree; and 120 credits at advanced level, equivalent to a master's degree. Candidates are able to gain credits through knowledge and training experiences. Credits can be accumulated over time, and transferred between different providers of the same qualification, and between qualifications.

There are 21 post-qualifying programmes with a child care and family focus; these are arranged by education and training consortia of agencies and colleges who negotiate, but not necessarily provide, training needs at both levels, approved by CCETSW. Candidates must hold DipSW or equivalent qualifications and submit evidence of any prior learning for which they are seeking credit.

As well as giving recognition to training for new functions, post-qualifying level credits are also useful for people returning to work who need to update or refresh their skills.

YOUTH AND COMMUNITY WORK

The National Youth Agency, which is government funded, is a partnership between central government, local education authorities and the voluntary sector; about 5,000 adults work full time in the youth services. The National Youth Agency is concerned with all aspects of initial and in-service training and educational needs for full-time youth and community workers; it produces a useful booklet *The NYA Guide to Initial Training Courses in Youth and Community Work* (available from NYA Sales Department, £4.50).

Part-time Youth Work

Part-time youth workers can get in touch with the local youth service, through the local education department, to find out about opportunities. Basic training is provided which can lead to nationally recognised NVQ qualifications. Part-time work can lead to becoming a full-time youth worker.

Professional Qualifications

Full-time courses include two-year certificate and diploma courses in youth and community work, three-year degree courses and full-time postgraduate courses.

There are also courses, known as apprenticeship schemes, for local people who normally do not have formal qualifications, but do have experience in youth and community work.

Applicants to courses other than degree courses must be aged at least 21 and have had experience of youth and community work, either paid or voluntary. Some certificate and diploma courses specify minimum entry requirements of five O levels or GCSEs, or equivalent; most also accept candidates who have relevant experience but no formal qualifications.

Other Forms of Qualification

No further training is necessary for qualification if the applicant is a teacher who achieved qualified status before the end of 1988; or has a social science diploma or degree started before 1977 and completed by 1981, with appropriate experience; or has relevant qualifications obtained overseas.

Full-time community courses

Bradford and Ilkley CC; Bristol, University of the West of England; Crewe and Alsager CHE; Derby U; Durham U; Goldsmiths C, Humberside U; University of London; Leeds Metropolitan U; Leicester, de Montfort U; Manchester Metropolitan U; North East Wales IHE (NEWI) at Cartrefle; Newman and Westhill Colleges; Reading U; Sunderland U; YMCA National C

Part-time courses
Cheltenham & Gloucester CHE; Greenwich U; De Montfort U, Leicester; Manchester Metropolitan U; Manchester U and Greater Manchester Community Work Training Group; Sunderland U; YMCA National C

Degree-only courses
Bradford and Ilkley Community C; Plymouth U; St Martin's C, Lancaster; Ulster U, Jordanstown

Part-time postgraduate courses
Brunel U; Greenwich U

Apprenticeship schemes
Bedfordshire, Buckinghamshire, Hertfordshire and Northamptonshire LEAs with Greenwich U; Dudley Metropolitan Borough Council; Turning Point with Goldsmith's C, London U

Validating learning from experience
Avon Accreditation Trust; Greater Manchester Community Work Training Group; North East Regional Training Group

Youth and Community Work in Scotland

The importance of youth and community work has long been acknowledged in Scotland, where it is generally known as community education. Training courses are run at four colleges of education, and the content of the courses is broadly in line with courses in the rest of the British Isles.

The qualifying degree is the BA in Community Education. All applicants for the three-year course are expected to have some previous experience of community education work. Many become interested in the career after working as a volunteer or part time for a few hours a week. This may be through contact with young people's projects or involvement with a local community group.

Normal minimum entry qualifications are three H-grade passes and one O-grade pass (band A, B or C) or one S grade at Level 1, 2 or 3 (passes to include English at H grade and a mathematical subject). Mature students who have completed Access courses or other non-traditional modes of study can also apply for the course. Opportunities also exist for entrants with appropriate experience but without formal academic qualifications.

Colleges offering the BA in Community Education
Moray House IE, Heriot-Watt U; Northern CE, Dundee; Strathclyde U

One-year Postgraduate Certificate in Community Education
Offered by the above colleges

Postgraduate Diploma in Community Education
A one-year full-time course or two-year part-time course is offered by
Edinburgh U.

All general enquiries about careers in community education should be
addressed to the Scottish Community Education Council.

Community and Youth Work Association YDA (Inc)

The YDA (see Useful Addresses) has several degrees of membership
– Fellowship, Membership, Associateship, Affiliateship – and
conducts an examination for its Diploma of Youth Development.
The YDA has standing liaison arrangements with other bodies in
the Youth Work, Play Work, Social Welfare, Leisure and Education
fields as a policy of cross-boundary support and training.

City and Guilds Youth Trainers' Award

C&G 9242 Youth Trainers' Award scheme is intended for instructors or supervisors on YT programmes. It is made up of four
separate modules: programme integration, working with young
people, assessment and reviewing, teaching skills; and courses are
organised to suit individual needs. YT instructors and others
wishing to follow a career in training can progress to the Certificate
in Training Competence (7254). Details are available from C&G.

Careers Guidance

To enter on a Diploma in Careers Guidance course you need one of
the following: (a) a recognised degree, (b) an approved diploma in
a subject such as social sciences, public administration, management studies, (c) a Diploma in Higher Education (or other diploma
of a comparable standard), (d) an equivalent professional qualification, (e) (if you are over 25) five years' relevant employment
experience. Candidates who are successful in the college interview
and likely to be able to reach the required academic standard do not
need to hold any award.

The training is in two parts: Part A is one year's full-time study
covering the principles and practice of guidance and counselling,
the study of education, training and employment. Successful
completion of Part A is certified by the Local Government Management Board; Part B is one year's in-service probation in a basic
grade as a careers officer. The full DCG is awarded on successful
completion of Parts A and B. For details write to the Local
Government Management Board (see Useful Addresses).

Discretionary grants are normally available from LEAs. In some
cases training awards are available through the college concerned
(particularly for those aged over 25). Some employment assistants,
after gaining work experience, are seconded to a course by an LEA.

Institutions offering diploma courses

Full-time courses
West of England U, Bristol; Huddersfield U; C of Guidance Studies, Swanley; Manchester Metropolitan U; Northumbria U at Newcastle upon Tyne; East London U; Paisley U; Strathclyde U; Reading U; Glamorgan U; University of Central England in Birmingham; Napier U, Edinburgh; Nottingham Trent U; South Bank U

Part-time courses
U of Central England in Birmingham; West of England U, Bristol; East London U; Huddersfield U; C of Guidance Studies, Swanley; Manchester Metropolitan U; Napier U, Edinburgh; Paisley U

PLAYWORK

Hospital Play Specialist Courses

The courses are designed to give additional training to people who are already working, or wishing to work, with children in acute, short-stay hospitals and specialising in play. The courses are of one year's duration and students attend colleges for three blocks of one week, one block of one week in a practical placement and one day a week in college between blocks.

Applicants must either hold a professional qualification (ie a Certificate of Education of an Institute of Education or the NNEB/ SNNB Diploma) or be a State Registered Nurse/Registered General Nurse or State Registered Children's Nurse/Registered Sick Children's Nurse, or have relevant qualifications/experience of working with children. No applicant under the age of 20 will be considered, as working with severely ill or disturbed children calls for a high degree of maturity. Selection for the few training places is by competitive interview.

The courses consist of lectures, discussion groups, seminars/ tutorials and include: child development, the value of play in a therapeutic setting and some instruction in basic medical/nursing techniques. Practical work includes art, craft, music and the making and adapting of play materials for sick children. There are hospital and other relevant visits.

The Hospital Play Specialist qualification is awarded to those students whose academic and practical work is deemed satisfactory after being subject to continuous assessment and who obtain a pass mark in a short written examination and undertake a special study on a subject of their own choice.

Course fees vary from college to college and are reviewed annually. In addition to the course fees there are the costs of essential books, stationery and visits to meet.

Courses are held at Bolton Metropolitan C; Stanmore C of Care &

Early Education, Bristol; Nescot, Ewell; North Warwickshire CTA, Nuneaton; Southwark C; Stevenson C, Edinburgh.

Further information can be obtained from the Hospital Play Staff Examination Board, address on page 110.

Playwork

The playwork profession is relatively new and historically, training provision has tended to be rather unstructured. However, there are now available a number of training opportunities at national and local levels, through short or longer-term courses.

City and Guilds NVQs in Playwork are now available at Levels 2 and 3, and an NVQ in Playwork Development at Level 4.

Two-year Full-time Diploma in Higher Education (Playwork)

Leeds Metropolitan U; Thurrock C; Norton C. Candidates under 21 need either five GCSE passes and two A-level passes or equivalent qualifications, such as BTEC and SYOCF (South Yorkshire Open College Federation) credits at Level IV; formal qualifications are not always necessary for those with relevant experience, though candidates must be able to cope with the formal study of the course. Contact the Playwork Team at each of these colleges for information about the course.

National Playwork Information Centre

The NPIC holds a library database which covers all aspects of play and recreation, including information on planning and designing children's play areas, safety at play, play and child development, theories of play, environmental play, legislation and play overseas.

In addition, a commercial database contains details of play-related businesses, such as manufacturers of play equipment and play consultants and services. The Information Centre also hosts IPA Resources (International Association for the Child's Right to Play), providing access to documents published overseas.

Network of National Centres for Playwork Education

There are four centres in the UK; part of their remit is to develop sources of information on courses following their own guidelines, and to participate in the development of training courses:

West Midlands Westhill, Weoley Park Road, Selly Oak, Birmingham B29 6LL
Cheltenham and the South West Cheltenham & Gloucester CHE, Francis Close Hall, Swindon Road, Cheltenham, Gloucestershire GL50 4AZ

London   Block D, Barnsbury Complex, Offord Road, London N1 1QG

North East   Kielder House, University of Northumbria, Coach Lane Campus, Coach Lane, Benton, Newcastle upon Tyne NE77 7XA.

For general information about a career in playwork, contact the Sports Council, Children's Play and Recreation, 359–361 Euston Road, London NW1 3AL.

Chapter 7

Useful Addresses and Where to Look for Jobs

Useful Addresses

Association of Community Workers, Grindon Lodge, Beech Grove Road, Newcastle upon Tyne NE4 2RS

Association of Nursery Training Colleges, The Princess Christian College, 26 Wilbraham Road, Fallowfield, Manchester M14 6JX

Barnardo's
Tanner's Lane, Barkingside, Ilford, Essex IG6 1QG
or 235 Corstorphine Road, Edinburgh EH12 7AR
or 542-544 Upper Newtownards Road, Belfast BT4 3HE

British Association of Domiciliary Care Officers, 2 Katherine's Close, Sindlesham, Wokingham, Berkshire RG11 5BZ

BTEC Information Office, Central House, Upper Woburn Place, London WC1H 0HH

CACHE, 8 Chequer Street, St Albans, Hertfordshire AL1 3XZ

Camp America, 37 Queen's Gate, London SW7 5HR

Central Council for Education and Training in Social Work
Derbyshire House, St Chad's Street, London WC1H 8AD
or 78-80 George Street, Edinburgh EH2 3BU
or Information Service, South Gate House, Wood Street, Cardiff CF1 1EW
or 6 Malone Road, Belfast BT9 5BN

Children's Society, Edward Rudolf House, 69-85 Margery Street, London WC1X 0JL

City and Guilds of London Institute, 1 Giltspur Street, London EC1A 9DD

Community and Youth Work Association, 122 Rochdale Road, Oldham, Lancashire OL1 1NT

Community and Youth Workers Union, Unit 202A, The Argent Centre, 60 Frederick Street, Hockley, Birmingham B1 3HS

Community Service Volunteers, 237 Pentonville Road, London N1 9NJ
or 22 High Street, Belfast BT1 2BD
or 236 Clyde Street, Glasgow G1 4JH

or Longstaff House, West Canal Wharf, Cardiff CF1 5DB

Elm House Christian Communications Ltd, 37 Elm Road, New Malden, Surrey KT3 3HB

Federation of Community Work Training Groups, 356 Glossop Road, Sheffield S10 7HR

Handicapped Adventure Playground Association, Fulham Palace, Bishops Avenue, London SW6 6EA

Handicapped Children in Hackney, Huddleston Centre, 30 Powell Road, London E5 8DJ

Hospital Play Staff Examination Board, Thomas Coram Foundation for Children, 40 Brunswick Square, London WC1N 1AZ

Institute of Careers Guidance, 27a Lower High Street, Stourbridge, West Midlands DY8 1TS

Institute of Leisure and Amenity Management, ILAM House, Lower Basildon, Reading RG8 9NE

Interchange Trust, Interchange Studios, Dalby Street, London NW5 3NQ

Local Government Opportunities, Local Government Management Board, 4th Floor, Arndale House, The Arndale Centre, Luton, Bedfordshire LU1 2TS

London Adventure Playground Association, 279 Whitechapel Road, London E1 1BY

NACRO New Careers Training, NACRO, 169 Clapham Road, London SW9 0PU

National Association for Maternal and Child Welfare, 40 Osnaburgh Street, London NW1 3ND

National Association for the Welfare of Children in Hospital, Argyle House, 29-31 Euston Road, London NW1 2SD

National Association of Boys' Clubs, 369 Kennington Lane, London SE11 5QY

National Association of Nursery Nurses, 10 Meriden Court, Great Clacton, Essex CO15 4XH

National Association for Voluntary Hostels, Fulham Palace, Bishops Avenue, London SW6 6EA

National Association of Youth and Community Education Officers, Cross Park, Ringmore, Kingsbridge, South Devon TQ7 4HW

National Children's Home, 85 Highbury Park, London N5 1UD

National Children's Play Information Centre, 359-361 Euston Road, London NW1 3AL and their Network of National Centres for Playwork Education (see page 107)

National Council for Voluntary Organisations, Regents Wharf, All Saints Street, London N1 9RL

National Council for Voluntary Youth Services, 3 Coborn Road, London E3 2DA

National Council of YMCAs, 640 Forest Road, Walthamstow, London E17 3DZ

National Federation of City Farms, 93 Whitby Road, Brislington, Bristol BS4 3QF

National Federation of Community Organisations, 8-9 Upper Street, Islington, London N1 0PR

National Play Information Centre, 359-361 Euston Road, London NW1 3AL

National Playing Fields Association, 25 Ovington Square, London SW3 1LQ

National Youth Agency, 17-23 Albion Street, Leicester LE1 6GD

Northern Ireland Pre-school Learning Alliance, Unit 3, Enterprise House, Eoucher Crescent, Eoucher Road, Belfast BT12 6HU

PGL Young Adventure Ltd, Adventure House, Station Street, Ross on Wye, Hereford & Worcester HR9 7AH

Play Matters - National Toy Libraries Association, 68 Church Way, London NW1 1LT

PPA (Pre-school Playgroups Association), Head Office, 61-63 King's Cross Road, London WC1X 9LL

Professional Association of Nursery Nurses, 77 Friar Gate, Derby DE1 1EZ

The Puppet Centre, Information and Resources, Battersea Arts Centre, Lavender Hill, London SW11 5TN

Save the Children Fund, Mary Datchelor House, 17 Grove Lane, London SE5 8SP

Scottish Community Education Council, Rosebery House, 9 Haymarket Terrace, Edinburgh EH12 5EZ

Scottish Council for Voluntary Organisations, 18-19 Claremont Crescent, Edinburgh EH7 4QD

Scottish Home and Health Department, Dover House, Whitehall, London SW1A 2AU

Scottish Nursery Nurses Board, 6 Kilnford Crescent, Dundonald, Kilmarnock, Ayrshire KA2 9DW

Scottish Pre-School Learning Alliance, 14 Elliot Place, Glasgow G3 8EP

SCOTVEC, Hanover House, 24 Douglas Street, Glasgow G2 7NG

Sports Council, 16 Upper Woburn Place, London WC1H 0QP

UCAS (Universities and Colleges Admission Service), Fulton House, Jessop Avenue, Cheltenham, Gloucestershire GL50 3SH

The Volunteer Centre, 356 Holloway Road, London N7 6PA

Volunteers Advisory Service, London Voluntary Service Council, 356 Holloway Road, London N7 6PA

Wales Council for Voluntary Action, Llys Ifor, Crescent Road, Caerphilly, Mid Glamorgan CF5 1XL

Wales Pre-School Learning Alliance Cymru, 2A Chester Street, Wrexham, Clwyd LL13 8BD

Youth Clubs UK, 11 St Bride Street, London EC4

Where to Look for Job Advertisements

Community Care
Daily Mail (local government posts on Wednesdays)
Guardian (Tuesdays and Wednesdays)
The Lady
New Statesman and Society
Nursery World
Nursing Times
Scan (from Scottish Community Education Council)
Social Work Today
The Times Educational Supplement
Youthwork (from Elm House Christian Communications Ltd)

You will find the names and addresses of authorities and organisations to whom you can write making your own general enquiries in the *Education Yearbook* and *Social Services Yearbook*.

The Scottish Community Education Council runs a Clearing House for youth posts in Scotland.

The Community and Youth Workers Union keeps information on vacant posts in England and Wales. You should state which part of the country you wish to work in when you enquire.